HOW THE WRIGHT BROTHERS GOT IT RIGHT

Cover photograph from the Library of Congress.

Wilbur and Orville Wright on the back porch of their home in Dayton Ohio, 1909. [From the Library of Congress.]

How the Wright Brothers Got it Right

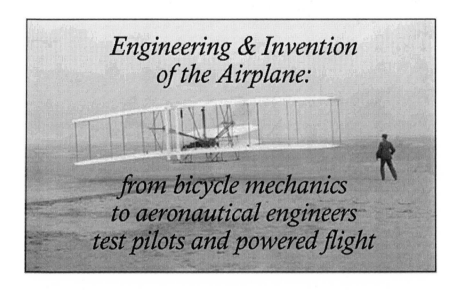

Engineering & Invention of the Airplane:

from bicycle mechanics to aeronautical engineers test pilots and powered flight

Jack L. Shagena, P.E. (Ret.)

Privately printed by the author

Printing 1 2 3 4 5 6 7 8 9 10

March 2007 – 250 copies

For Copies:

Jack L. Shagena, Jr.
2017 Gumtree Terrace
Bel Air, Maryland 21015-6035

Tel: 410 569 0988

jshagena@comcast.net
http://home.comcast.net/~jshagena/home.html

ISBN 9780977686650

Library of Congress Control Number: 2006908164

Printed in the U.S.A.
InstantPublisher.com

Foreword

If the preparation of a manuscript ever needed adherence to a guiding principle, it was this book – writing the understandable story of *how* the Wright brothers achieved first flight. To do this, the overriding mandate penned in each paragraph, illuminated in every illustration, and clarified in each caption has been:

KISS – Keep It Short & Simple.

Therein lies a challenge for the writer, for what the Wright brothers achieved in inventing the airplane was far from simple. To explain it in an easy-to-follow way required insight into their thinking as they transitioned from bicycle mechanics, to aeronautical engineers, to test pilots, to powered flight. Not too surprisingly, perhaps, these requisite understandings are found in their own recorded words as they wrote letters, presented papers, gave interviews, were deposed, and in the process actually revealed *how* their earth-shattering feat was accomplished.

Therefore, it was necessary to look beyond the words to glean the clues as to how their minds logically and methodically proceed along the right TRAC of: **T**esting and retesting; **R**ecognizing problems; **A**nalyzing solutions; and **C**reating a workable approach.

This is the essential essence of good engineering and despite the Wright brothers' lack of formal training, they intrinsically understood this four-step methodology and meticulously applied it. You are about to learn the secrets of their success.

3

Contents

5

Preface

With more than two-dozen books already published about the Wright brothers, the inquiring reader will wonder what possible need would a new biography fulfill? The answer is simple – using an insightful engineering perspective, explore the synergistic, perhaps symbiotic, minds of two truly great inventors who used a disciplined and methodical approach to evolve the airplane, a feat that heretofore had befuddled the best thinkers of the day. Therefore, this effort can be more accurately described as a techography.

Herein is chronicled the Wrights amazing story, which is frequently told by participants Wilbur and Orville in the first person. As they wrote almost a century ago using some terminology that has changed over time, occasionally an explanation is needed to relate their message to the present-day reader. This has been done with a combination of text and graphics that clarifies often-complicated concepts in easy-to-understand terms.

When examining the accomplishments of the Wright's, three things come to mind: control, control, and control. First and most importantly was the three-dimensional airborne control of the wing that supported the gliders they initially tested and flew. Second, it was the meticulous control of wind tunnel experiments, which provided accurate data used in later designs of the wings and airfoils. And third, the piloting control learned in glider tests was essential to confidently demonstrating heavier-than-air powered flight to a skeptical public.

They achieved all this through an insightful understanding of the real problems faced, through a determined and dedicated effort, and through knowledge they discovered along the way with the help of their corresponding friend and silent cheerleader, Octave Chanute.

This is their story of engineering, innovation, and inventions told for the very first time in an easy to understand way for all readers – including those with no technical training.

Acknowledgements

In the preparation of this book, access to primary documentation was essential, so many thanks to the Library of Congress for scanning and placing online their collection of Wright brothers written information and photographs. In 1953, Marvin W. McFarland edited *The Papers of Wilbur and Orville Wright*, which transcribed much of the their correspondence, diaries, and notes. McFarland's insightful footnotes to many of the documents were most valuable.

Since the Wrights accomplished their groundbreaking flight in 1903, there have been many biographies published about their lives. None, however, was as perceptive as *The Bishop's Boys* written by Tom D. Crouch in 1989. Crouch's dedication to ferret out the most obscure details and weave them into an engaging narrative is a superb work.

Other biographies I found useful were *Visions of a Flying Machine*, 1990, by Peter L. Jakab; *One Day at Kitty Hawk*, 1975, by John Evangelist Walsh; and *The Wright Brothers: A Biography Authorized by Orville Wright*, 1943, by Fred C. Kelly.

Historian, Darrell Collins, at the Wright Brothers National Monument at Kitty Hawk was kind enough to read a copy of the manuscript and provided many comments, which made the book more accurate.

I was fortunate to be able to exchange emails with recognized aviation expert Fred E. C. Culick, who critiqued selected portions of the manuscript and provided valuable feedback. Good friend William T. "Bill" Sisson read an early draft and offered suggestions for making the presentation easier to understand.

Once again, copyeditor Erika Compton read the draft and corrected a number of things that had escaped the author's eye.

Finally, thanks to my loving wife, Signe, who listened patiently as I rambled on about the progress and problems in writing such a book. As they say in Baltimore, "love you, Hon."

Jack L. Shagena, Jr. developed an interest in history at an early age while accompanying his parents on visits to Colonial Williamsburg. He graduated from Virginia Polytechnic Institute in 1959, with a bachelor's degree in electrical engineering and in 1966 received a master's degree in management science from Johns Hopkins University. He worked as an engineer, program manager, and aerospace executive for Bendix, later AlliedSignal, for thirty-four years. Upon retiring in 1993, he began researching Colonial and federal history and wrote his first book, *Brief History & Walking Tour of Historic Chesapeake City,* a former lock town along the nineteenth-century Chesapeake and Delaware Canal.

When researching and writing the script for an audiotape, *Historic Driving Tour of Cecil County,* a chance discovery of a Maryland roadside historic marker identified someone other than Robert Fulton as the inventor of the steamboat. His interest in history and engineering background coalesced and his book, *Who Really Invented the Steamboat? Fulton's* Clermont *Coup,* was published by Prometheus in June 2004.

Mr. Shagena, a retired registered professional engineer, has also written, *An Illustrated History of the Barrel in America; Jerusalem – A Restored Mill Village, An Illustrated History of Tinware in America; Bel Air Roller Mills: The Town's First Industry; Eden Mill: An Illustrated History;* and a fun book, *Things Your Grandparents Used to Say: the Wise, the Witty, and the Weird.*

He and his wife, Signe, have eleven grandchildren and live in Harford County near Bel Air, Maryland.

Chapter 1

Earlier Aerial Experiments Perused

I am well convinced that Ariel Navigation will form a most prominent feature in the progress of civilization.

– Sir George Cayley, 1804

Flight close to the earth is made possible by a thin layer of atmosphere that constantly moves around on the surface being held down by gravity. Since the air has mass, it has weight, and produces a pressure of about fifteen pounds per square inch near the earth's surface, but gradually dissipates at higher elevations of several miles. As a result, the layer is very thin relative to the earth's size and can be imagined by considering the planet to be a tennis ball and the protruding fuzz as the earth's atmosphere.

Fanciful Flight

Man, since seeing the first bird fly, has dreamed of making travel easier and taking to the air. For thousands of years this vision was only fanciful thought as early experimenters unsuccessfully attempted flight by flapping wings akin to the birds. Such heavier-than-air flying machines are called ornithopters.

About 1700 BC, according to Greek mythology, a young man, Icarus, made wings out of wax and feathers and flew out of imprisonment on his way to freedom. As the story is told, he failed to listen to his father and flew too close to the sun. This caused the wax to melt and when the feathers fell out, he suddenly fell to his death.

About three millenniums later c.1400, the world's greatest scientist, artist, and engineer of the time, Leonardo da Vinci, sketched a number of plans for flying machines. He devoted much thought to flight – he is said to have produced some 500 drawings and written 35,000 words on the subject of aeronautics. Some of his work was quite detailed, as he possessed the eye of a painter and the mind of an engineer. He observed birds and tried to replicate their wings for human flight, but was unsuccessful.

A locksmith, Monsier Besnier, living in Sable, France, in 1678 invented one of the more interesting and easily understood flying devices. A pair of wings, each pivoted on the shoulder of a man and moved up and  down by hands and feet, was intriguingly simple. When the wing moved upward, it folded together, reopening when the direction was reversed. It is reported he sold a pair of wings to a passing entertainer, but such a flying method could not have been remotely successful.[1]

Practically, it was impossible for man to fly without auxiliary power, as his own power was not even remotely suited for the task. "His heart represents only 0.5 percent of his total weight, whereas that of the golden eagle is over 8 percent and the tiny hummingbird up to 22 percent. Compared to man's normal heartbeat of 70 times a minute, even that of a sparrow throbs at a fantastic 800 times a minute in flight."[2] (Nevertheless, in 1979, using strong lightweight materials, Paul MacCready, Jr. built and flew the *Gossamer Condor* over a one-mile figure-eight course. Two years later he piloted the *Gossamer Albatross* over the English Channel, a distance of twenty miles.)[3]

Toward a More Analytical Approach

George Cayley was born in 1773 into a moderately prosperous family and spent much of his life working in the field of what we call today aeronautics. He made a number of important contributions, recognizing the forces that impact an airplane are: lift, drag, thrust, and gravity. When discussing lift he noted, "The whole [flight] problem is confined within these limits, *viz.* To make a surface [wing] support a given weight by the application of power to the resistance of air."[4] Cayley wrote a major paper titled "On Aerial Navigation," which was published in three parts in *Nicholson's Journal* in 1808. Because of this work and other contributions, he is sometimes called the Father of Aviation.

Otto Lilienthal was born in 1848 and educated at what is now the Technical University of Berlin. As a trained engineer who had a successful career in developing steam engines for nautical use, he brought respectability to soaring on gliders. He pioneered the concept, later used by brothers Wilbur and Orville Wright, that "One can get a proper insight into the practice of flying only by actual flying experiments."[5]

Lilienthal published a book translated as *Birdflight as a Basis for Aviation*, which contained tables for lift that were initially used by the Wrights. After making about 2,000 flights, one of his gliders stalled on August 9, 1896 and he crashed and died the next day.

Octave Chanute was born in Paris in 1832 and came to the United States in 1836 when his father accepted the position of vice president of a college in Louisiana. He went to work as a railroad surveyor in 1849 and through a series of promotions specialized in bridge construction winning distinction for his work. He semi-retired in 1888 and began a comprehensive study of aeronautical experiments. He collected all the available data and between 1891 and 1893 this information was published in as series of articles in the *Railroad and Engineering Journal*. In 1894 they were published in book form with the title *Progress in Flying Machines.*[6]

This book would become a major resource for the Wrights and Wilbur would contact Chanute in May 1900 to begin a long series of letters with occasional visits. Chanute would play an important role in providing sage advice on practical matters, but with regard to the aeronautical theory developed by the Wright, Chanute was very quickly out of his element. The letters and visits did contribute greatly their success, as will be noted throughout the rest of the book.

[1] Bill Gunston, editor-in-chief, *Aviation: Year by Year* (London: Dorling Kindersley, Ltd., 2001), p. 14.

[2] John W. R. Taylor and Kenneth Munson, *History of Aviation* (New York: Crown Publishers, Inc, 1972), p. 11.

[3] "Human-Powered Transportation." *The New Book of Popular Science*. Grolier Online http://nbps.grolier.com/cgi-bin/article?assettype=t&assetid=a4030 800-h; February 1, 2007.

[4] As found in http://www.aerodyn.org/People/cayley.html; September 2, 2006.

[5] As quoted by Richard P. Hallion, Historical Advisor to the Air force Centennial of Flight Office, found at http://www.af.mil/history/ottolilienthal.asp; September 2, 2006.

[6] From the introduction by Joshua Stoff in Octave Chanute, *Progress in Flying Machines* (1894, reprint; Mineola NY: Dover Publications, Inc., 1977), pp. iii–iv.

Chapter 2

1892 – Getting Started in Dayton, Ohio

*For some years now I have been afflicted with
the belief that flight is possible to man. My
disease has increased in severity and I feel it
will soon cost me an increased amount of
money if not my life.*

– Wilbur Wright, May 1900

By 1892, brothers Orville and Wilbur Wright had transitioned
from a newspaper and printing business to owners of the Wright
Cycle Company in Dayton, Ohio. They were doing well riding the
popularity craze that started in the late 1880s with the "safety"
bicycle. They sold new bicycles, rented them, repaired broken ones,
and by 1896 were manufacturing two models called the Van Cleve
and the St. Clair.

These made-to-order bicycles were fabricated from "high-
grade materials throughout" and initially sold for $60 to $65 and
$42.50 respectively, at a time when competing brands were being
offered by Montgomery Ward & Company for $40 to $50.[1] This
experience in producing a reliable and quality product would bode
well for their venture into building an airplane.

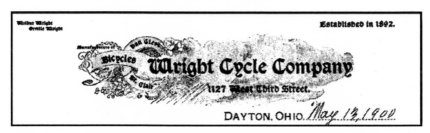

Figure 2-1. Letterhead of the Wright Bicycle Company is shown with an
address of 1127 West Third Street, which was occupied by them in 1897.
[From the Library of Congress.]

Their shop included an array of equipment, including a turret lathe, drill press, tube cutting equipment, and a homemade electrical welder. There was a line shaft with pulleys and belts in the ceiling to power the machinery, which in turn was driven by a single-cylinder gasoline engine.

At this time, before the turn of the twentieth century, the country's fascination with bicycles and airplanes prompted writers to draw parallels. The editor of one newspaper remarked, "The flying machine will not be the same shape, or at all in the style of the numerous kinds of cycles, but the study to produce a light, swift machine is likely to lead to an evolution in which wings will play a conspicuous part."[2] Others also equated cycling with flying, perhaps because of the speed and light-weightiness required or it may have been the inherent instability of both machines. Historian Tom Crouch, writing about the Wright brothers noted, "The manned glider was the aeronautical equivalent of the bicycle."[3] This is a concept that is worth examining, as it will provide insight into many of the problems that faced by the Wrights.

Figure 2-2. A "safety" bicycle of the type ridden by the Wright brothers around Dayton, Ohio is shown. [From *The Sears, Roebuck and Co. Catalogue* (1902, reprint; New York: Bounty Books, 1969), page 277.]

As every rider knows, the bicycle can fall from side to side and, when moving, may turn in an unpredictable manner unless steered by the rider. It is therefore unstable in two directions. Once

14

moving, however, the spinning wheels provide some gyroscopic stability for the left and right (lateral) balance, but when the bicycle leans to one side, the rider must always be prepared to steer in the same direction to bring the vehicle to vertical. The predecessor of the two equal-sized, or nearly equal-sized, wheels used on the "safety" bicycle was the so-called penny farthing shown in figure 2-3. Here the two wheels were of significantly different size and it was not uncommon for the smaller one to lift off the ground, effectively turning the bicycle into a unicycle, and making it more difficult to control.

Figure 2-3. A seventeen-year-old boy, in cycling attire, stands before his new bicycle about 1883. This bicycle required much more skill to ride than today's bikes. [Photo of Dayton C. Miller from the Library of Congress.]

Consider for a moment that the smaller wheel has been removed, turning the device into unicycle. Now the rider would find he is unstable in yet another direction. He can fall forward or backward, fall left or right, or rotate around the point the single tire meets the riding surface. Rather than having two dimensions of instability with the bicycle, he now has three, a more realistic analogy of the airplane. More about this parallel is discussed in chapter 3.

Wilbur Ponders His Future

The Wrights father, Milton, lent his two sons money to start the bicycle business, and from time to time they would apprise him of its status. As with most business ventures, there were ups and downs and increased competition caused Wilbur to think about whether he was headed in the right professional direction. He considered going to college and pursuing a different career, but would need some financial help. At age twenty-seven he sent this letter to his dad, somewhat tentatively seeking advice and support:

> I have thought about it more or less for a number of years but my health has been such that I was afraid that it might be time and money wasted to do so, but I have felt so much better for a year or so that I have thought more seriously of it and have decided to see what you think of it and would advise.
>
> I do not think I am specially fitted for success in any commercial pursuit even if I had the proper personal and business references to assist me. . . . I have always thought I would like to be a teacher. Although there is no hope of attaining such financial success as might be attained in some of the other professions or in commercial pursuits, yet it is an honorable pursuit, the pay is sufficient to live comfortably and happily, and is less subject to uncertainties than almost any other occupation. It would be congenial to my tastes and I think with proper training I could be reasonably successful.[4]

Wilbur, well into the third decade of his life in 1894, had not yet found his calling. He had followed his brother, Orville, into the newspaper publishing, job printing, then the bicycle business, but had not established his own identity. His father would respond positively to furthering his education, but Wilbur was still not ready to move in that direction.

Otto Lilienthal Dies

The death of a German mechanical engineer five thousand miles away would seem to have portended little impact on two bicycle mechanics in Dayton, Ohio. But this was not the case, at least for Wilbur. To understand the connection it is only necessary to read what the brothers wrote in 1909 about how a small toy kindled an "abiding" interest in flight:

> Though the subject of aërial navigation is generally considered new, it has occupied the minds of men more or less from the earliest ages. Our personal interest in it dates from our childhood days. Late in the autumn of 1878, our father came into the house one evening with some object partly concealed in his hands, and before we could see what it was, he tossed it into the air. Instead of falling to the floor, as we expected, it flew across the room till it struck the ceiling where it fluttered awhile, and finally sank to the floor. It was a little toy, known to scientist as a "hélicoptère," but which we, with sublime disregard for science, at once dubbed a "bat." It was a light frame of cork and bamboo, covered with paper, which formed two screws, driven in opposite directions by rubber bands under torsion. A toy so delicate lasted only a short time in the hands of small boys, but its memory was abiding.[5]

"Its memory was abiding" summarizes the indelible imprint a clever toy or bit of fascinating information can impart to young minds.[6] From other descriptions provided by the Wrights, we learn this toy (shown at the right), was a M. Pénaud flying screw, invented about 1870, with two lightweight counter-rotating blades.

Several years after receiving the toy, the brothers tried to construct larger models, which failed to perform as well as the original. Later they were to learn the reason: "a machine having only twice the linear dimensions of another would require eight times the power."[7] They did, however, build kites and became so adept at flying them they were regarded as experts. As they grew older, however, the sport became "unbecoming to boys of our ages" so they gave it up.

Wilbur believed the death of the German engineer was a turning point in his life and triggered in his mind an interest in reading about the subject of flight, followed by giving it serious thought, then to actual experimentation – all innate characteristics of a good engineer. Thinking back years later, he would write:

> My own active interest in aeronautical problems dates back to the death of Lilienthal in 1896. The brief notice of his death which appeared in the telegraphic news at that time aroused a passive interest which had existed from my childhood, and led me to take down from the shelves of our home library a book on *Animal Mechanism* by Prof. Marey, which I had already read several times. From this I was led to read more modern works, and as my brother soon became equally interested with myself, we soon passed from the reading to the thinking, and finally to the working stage. It seemed to us that the main reason why the problem had remained so long unsolved was that no one had been able to obtain any adequate practice.[8]

Otto Lilienthal was a mechanical engineer and part-time glider pioneer who had tested fifteen monoplanes and three biplanes from 1891 until 1896, when a flying accident took his life.

During the course of approximately two thousand test flights (see figure 2-4), Lilienthal had accumulated piloting experience and also conducted experiments to catalog lifting data for various wing shapes that he compiled in tables. The Wright brothers would initially use this information to design the wings of their flyer.

The news of his death, however, did not immediately translate in activity by either of the Wright brothers. At that time Orville was bedridden with typhoid fever, a struggle that lasted for six weeks, and Wilbur was still contemplating his future. In the interim, for both brothers, the bicycle business would be their primary focus.

Shown on the right is a claim ticket, given to people who left their bicycle at the Wright Cycle Company for repair. [From the Library of Congress.]

WRIGHT CYCLE Co.

Repair Department.

We guarantee all work; but complaint must be made promptly.

Storage will be charged on all wheels not called for in ten days.

KEEP THIS CARD.

No. 1 0 3 9

Figure 2-4. Otto Lilienthal jumps off a launching platform testing a glider configuration. [From Octave Chanute, *Progress in Flying Machines* (1894, reprint; Mineola, NY: Dover Publications, 1977), page 276.]

Pondering Then Action

For more than two years thereafter, Wilbur was in a prolonged period of gestation – thinking about whether he could make a contribution to heavier-than-air flight. Orville recalled some two decades later: "In the early spring of 1899, our interest in the subject [flight] was again aroused through the reading of a book on ornithology."[9]

This statement is interesting, as when Wilbur wrote a letter to the Smithsonian Institution on May 30 of that year soliciting information, it was written in the first person singular. Up to that time the brothers had always spoken of "we" and shortly thereafter this pronoun would characteriz all of their public writing and comment. It appears, however, when the letter was penned, Wilbur clearly became the leader of the team, but in all public forums thereafter each presented the results as a joint product of the pair.

Wilbur's Smithsonian letter of inquiry (see figure 2-5) began:

I have been interested in the problem of mechanical and human flight ever since as a boy I constructed a number of' bats of various sizes after the style of Cayley's and Penaud's machines. My observations since have only convinced me more firmly that human flight is possible and practicable. It is only a question of knowledge and skill just as in all acrobatic feats. Birds are the most perfectly trained gymnasts in the world and are specially well fitted for their work, and it may lie that man will never equal them, but no one who has watched a bird chasing an insect or another bird can doubt that feats are performed which require three or four times the effort required in ordinary flight. I believe, that simple flight at least is possible to man and that the experiments and investigations of a large number of independent workers will result in the accumulation of information and knowledge and skill which will finally lead to accomplished flight.

WRIGHT CYCLE COMPANY

1127 West Third Street.

Dayton, Ohio, May 30, 1899.

The Smithsonian Institution,

Washington.

Dear Sirs:

I have been interested in the problem of mechanical and human flight ever since as a boy I constructed a number of bats of various sizes after the style of Cayley's and Penaud's machines. My observations since have only convinced me more

Figure 2-5. Portion of the letter Wilbur Wright sent to the Smithsonian Institution asking for information about flight. [From the Library of Congress.]

Wilbur's confidence permeates the first paragraph. To him, after giving the matter careful thought, it was not a question of whether flight was possible, but when. Humbly, he did not suggest he had the answers; only the accumulated knowledge of many independent investigators would lead to success. He continued:

I am about to begin a systematic study of the subject in preparation for practical work to which I expect to devote what time I can spare from my regular business. I wish to obtain such papers as the Smithsonian Institution has published on this subject, and if possible a list of other works in print in the English language. I am an enthusiast, but not a crank in the sense that I have some pet theories as to the proper construction of a flying machine. I wish to avail myself of all that is already known and then if possible add my mite to help on the future worker who will attain final success.[10]

As an emerging engineer ready to begin a systematic study, Wilbur knew instinctively he "didn't want to reinvent the wheel" and his first assignment was to study with an open mind – not with predisposed "pet theories" – all the work that had already been accomplished. He was not prepared to learn French or German so he carefully specified he was interested in documents written only in English.

Lastly, he was willing to add his "mite to help on the future worker" believing he would not achieve success in his lifetime. He underestimated his own intellectual capacity and was fortunate Orville joined him in the enterprise, making his engineering efforts significantly more productive.

The secretary of the Smithsonian sent him some information and noted he could acquire additional reports for $1. Wilbur ordered these, on which the 1989 Wright biographer Tom Crouch noted:

It was the most important exchange of correspondence in the history of the Smithsonian. The receipt of those pamphlets set in motion a chain of events that would culminate in the invention of the aircraft.[11]

Wilbur had found a good match for his self-proclaimed innate talents that "excelled other men" in the challenge of engineering heavier-than-air flight. He was thirty-two years old and, having a keen assessment of his potential, believed this opportunity would prove to the world what his intellect, industry, and perseverance could accomplish. He needed to confront something big to prove to himself he was the measure of the task. The aircraft, he firmly believed, was it.

An Elegantly Simple Idea

The Wrights figured the total time Lilienthal had actually spent gliding was about five hours spread over five years, and this was done in bursts of ten seconds. Such an approach to learn how to ride a bicycle, something they were very familiar with, led them to conclude this was not practical. To learn to pilot a glider, they thought, would require practice sessions that lasted perhaps as long as one hour. They believed a properly constructed glider in a wind of eighteen miles per hour should be able to support a man's weight and allow for sustained periods of tests.

Lilienthal had used the positioning of his hanging body to stabilize a glider when it was perturbed by a gust of wind. Wilbur immediately recognized this could only work for small airframes where the pilot's own weight could be effective in counter balancing unpredictable air currents.

Wilbur began to watch birds in flight more carefully. They had no effective way to shift their weight, but nevertheless were able to balance themselves and quickly adjust to changes in air currents. He concluded their "balance was controlled by utilizing dynamic reactions" of quickly "turning the forward edge of one wingtip up and the other down."[12] The question presented to his inquiring mind was how to accomplish a corresponding reaction on an airfoil built by man? The answer came to him unexpectedly when he picked up an empty rectangular pasteboard box, which had contained a bicycle inner tube. Orville tells the story:

> Wilbur showed me a method of getting the same results [turning wing edges] as we had contemplated in our first idea without the structural defect of the original. He demonstrated the method by means of a pasteboard box, which had the two of the opposite ends removed. By holding the top corner forward and the rear lower corner on one end of the box between his thumb and forefinger and the rear upper corner and the lower forward corner of the other in like manner, and by pressing the corners together the upper and lower surface of the box were given a helicoidal twist, presenting the top and bottom surfaces of the box at different angles on the right and left sides.[13]

Wilbur perceptively saw in his mind's eye the upper and lower wing on a biplane being manipulated in a manner analogous to the way birds controlled their attitude in flight (see figure 2-6).

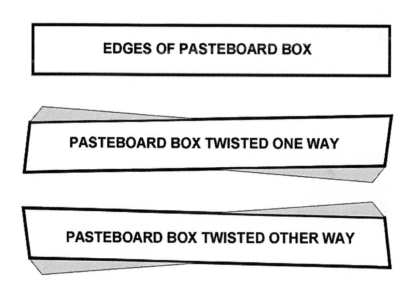

Figure 2-6. Slightly squeezing opposite end corners of a pasteboard box, the edges could be made to rise either on the left or right, portending a solution to lateral stability for an aircraft wing. [Illustrations by the author from construction of a model, 2006.]

> *At this moment was born the practical realization of the secret of lateral (roll) aircraft control. Early on it would be called wing twisting or warping, but was really the invention of the aircraft aileron.*

The twisting intuitively appeared to be the way to lateral control, but would it work? A test would provide the answer. The brothers constructed a bi-wing kite, five feet long tip to tip and about thirteen inches wide. Two pairs of tethering strings were arranged to raise or lower the leading edges of the flat surfaces. Their design is shown in figures 2-7 and 2-8.

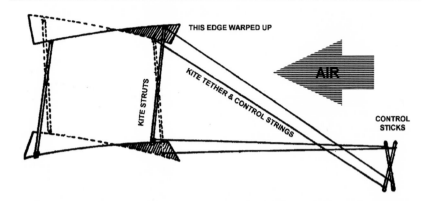

Figure 2-7. Holding a control stick in either hand, Wilbur was able to change the angle at which the leading edge of the left- or right-side wing met the oncoming air. Thus, he was able to confirm this approach provided the lateral (roll) stability to keep the kite level. [Illustration from Marvin W. McFarland, editor, *The Papers of Wilbur and Orville Wright* (1953, reprint; McGraw-Hill, 2001), page 10, annotated by the author.]

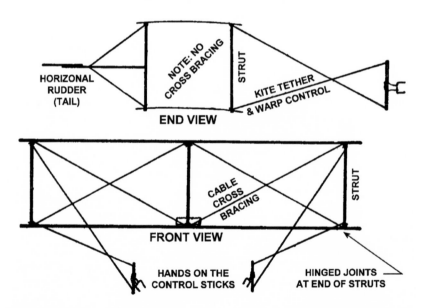

Figure 2-8. Front and end views of the bi-plane kite and control strings the Wright brothers used to demonstrate the effectiveness of wing warping to achieve effective lateral (roll) control. [Illustration from McFarland, *Papers*, page 9, annotated by the author.]

The innovativeness of his design can be better understood from the two-part figure 2-8. The top portion shows how the crossed tether lines attached to the end of the control stick allowed the wings to be warped by moving his wrist forward and backward. A fixed tail stabilized the kite fore and aft (pitch).

Shown in the front view of the figure is how the two bi-kite surfaces were held apart by the struts and held together by the cable cross bracing, akin to the construction of a bridge truss. Missing, however, were such cable cross bracings on the ends, so the wings could be warped like the pasteboard box shown in figure 2-6 and the kite in figure 2-7. Wing warping was an elegantly simple idea that found a very practical application in lateral or roll control of a flying wing.

The next step was to build a glider capable of supporting a man's weight that could be used to learn the secrets of piloting. This would be far more difficult than a kite, but as the reader will discover in the next chapter, the brothers were up to the challenge.

Shown on the left is Wilbur, who strikes a rather serious poise for his childhood portrait. Orville, age nine and one-half, is on the right. [From the Library of Congress.]

[1] Tom Crouch, *The Bishop's Boys: The Life of Wilbur and Orville Wright* (New York: W. W. Norton & Co., 1989), p. 113; and Montgomery Wards & Co. *Fall & Winter Catalogue & Buyers Guide, No. 56* (1894-95, reprint; Chicago: Follett Publishing Co., 1970), p. 536.

[2] Editor of the Binghamton, NY, *Republican* on June 4, 1896, p. 114, as quoted in Crouch, *Bishop's Boys,*

[3] Ibid., p. 115.

[4] Ibid., p. 110.

[5] Orville and Wilbur Wright, "The Wright Brothers' Aëroplane," *The Century Magazine* (Sept. 1908) 76: 641.

[6] My seventh grade teacher presented me a sealed lead-acid battery with a charger. It was the diameter of a D-cell battery, but twice as long and provided the renewable energy to power a variety of buzzers, electromagnets, and other experiments that led me to a career in electrical engineering.

[7] Orville and Wilbur Wright, "Aëroplane," p. 641.

[8] Martin W. McFarland, ed., *The Papers of Wilbur and Orville Wright*, 2 vols. (1953, reprint; New York: McGraw Hill, 2001) 1:103.

[9] Crouch, *Bishop's Boys*, p. 160.

[10] McFarland, *Papers*, pp. 4–5.

[11] Crouch, *Bishop's Boys*, p. 162.

[12] Ibid., p. 172.

[13] From a January 13, 1920 deposition of Orville Wright as found in McFarland, *Papers*, p. 8.

Chapter 3

1900 – Building and Testing a Glider

To design one is nothing,
To build one is easy,
To fly one is everything.

– Attributed to Otto Lilienthal

S afety was always a priority to Wilbur. Otto Lilienthal had died as a result of a glider accident in 1896 and three years later the same fate had befallen to another glider experimenter, Englishman Perry Pilcher. Writing in 1908, the brothers made this observation about piloting a heavier-than-air machine: "The balancing of a flyer may seem, at first thought, to be a very simple matter, yet almost every experimenter has found in this the one point which he could not satisfactorily master."[1]

In another publication earlier the same year, a similar concern had been identified and presented this way:

> At that time (1900) there was really only one problem remaining to be solved to make a workable flying-machine – the problem of equilibrium. Men already knew how to make aeörplanes that would support them when driven through the air at sufficient speed, and there were engines light enough per horse-power to propel the aeörplanes at the necessary speed, and to carry their own weight and the weight of an operator. There were plenty of aeörplanes that would fly in still air. What was needed was an airship that would not capsize when the wind was blowing.[2]

The secret of designing an airplane with the necessary controls to allow a pilot to stabilize the craft when encountering turbulent air, had escaped the serious attention of previous experimenters. Some mistakenly believed that a flying wing, after being perturbed by a wind gust, would simply level out and self-stabilize, akin to a boat after experiencing turbulent water. This was definitely not the case and this design challenge became the Wright brother's primary focus over the next half decade.

The Instability Challenge

To comprehend the difficulties faced by the Wright brothers, it is worthwhile to first examine an easier-to-understand parallel found in the unicycle first introduced in chapter 2. Two views of the device are shown in figure 3-1.

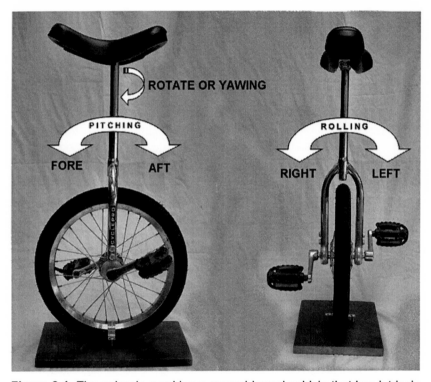

Figure 3-1. The unicycle provides a ground-based vehicle that has intrinsic instability characteristics similar to those of the airplane. [Photographs and annotations by the author, 2006.]

When a rider seated in the saddle uses his legs to hold the pedals in a fixed position, the device is unstable forward and backward rotating or *pitching* around the point the tire meets the pavement. This same instability exists in the aircraft with the supporting wing tends to rotate around its longitudinal center of gravity. The unicycle can also lean to the rider's right and left, akin to the airplane's lateral or *rolling* instability when confronted with a gust of air. The single wheel can also rotate on its tire clockwise or in the opposite direction depending on the action of the rider. This is called *yaw*. When a turning aircraft slips sideways, as the tire could on ice, it is called *adverse yaw*.

Regarding the aircraft's pitch stability, the small arrows on the bottom of the wing in figure 3-2 are the results of the air moving across the lower surface at a small, so-called angle of attack. Consolidating all of these into one large arrow, called the center of pressure, is the composite or result of all the smaller ones. If the center of pressure lines up the center of gravity (that point on which the wing, including the attached airframe, will balance), the surface is pushed upward and no rotational force will be produced. With changes in angle of attack, however, the center of pressure will move, thus introducing fore and aft or pitch instability.

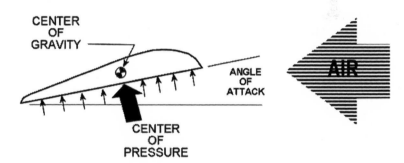

Figure 3-2. Cross-section of an aircraft wing showing the effects of moving air on producing an upward pressure or lift. [Illustration by the author, 2006.]

In 1900, the Wrights experimented with a lateral or roll balance technique recommended by some earlier fliers that was:

> arranging the wings in the shape of a broad V, to form a dihedral angle, with the center low and the wing-tips elevated. In theory this was an automated system, but in practice it had two serious defects: first, it tended to keep the machine oscillating; and, second its usefulness was restricted to calm air.[3]

They concluded therefore, "Control was much easier after we made it [the wing] straight."[4] Also they were aware that fore and aft or pitch balance had been attempted using an aft tail:

In a slightly modified form the same system was applied to the fore-and-aft balance. The main aeörplane was set at a positive angle, and a horizontal tail at a negative angle, while the center of gravity was placed forward. As in the case of lateral control, there was a tendency to constant undulation, and the very forces which caused a restoration of balance in calms, caused a disturbance of balance in winds.[5]

A better idea was needed, so it occurred to them, "We would arrange the machine so that it would not tend to right itself. We would make it as inert as possible to the effects of change in direction or speed, and thus reduce the effect of wind-gust to a minimum."[6] They concluded that wing warping could be at the command of the pilot to correct for lateral movement, and they could achieve fore and aft or roll stability by using a forward rudder turned in the same direction of the wing. The pilot, lying down on the lower wing, would move a lever to adjust the rudder and move his feet, later hips, left or right to control the warp or twisting in the wings.

Designing the Glider

Now the problem facing them was the dimensions of the flying machine to carry the weight of the structure, estimated to be fifty pounds, plus the one hundred forty pound weight of either of them as a pilot. Some science was known and it was put to work. Effectively, all of the weight had to be borne by the wings and its area could be determined by recognizing the lifting capacity (L) was proportional to several factors, or so-called parameters:

Surface Area of the Wing (S) – the lifting capacity of the flying machine was directly related the area of the wing, or for a bi-plane, both wings.

Velocity of the Air Squared (V^2) – the lifting capacity was proportional to the air velocity squared. This comes about as a doubling of the velocity causes the wing to encounter twice as many particles of air in a given time, and each particle has twice the impact. The brothers decided to base the design on a headwind of fifteen miles per hour.

Coefficient of Lift (C_L) – the lifting capacity of a wing as determined from a table prepared by Otto Lilienthal was used. For a ten-degree angle of attack, the value was found to be 0.825.[7]

Coefficient of Air Pressure (k) – the factor for air pressure, which varied with altitude and temperature but for flights close to the earth was relatively constant, and was initially determined to be 0.005.

The equation for lift was: $L = S \times V^2 \times C_L \times k$

Therefore: 190 (total weight) $= S \times 15^2 \times 0.825 \times 0.005$

Solving the equation: $S = 190 / (225 \times 0.825 \times 0.005)$

Hence: $S = 204.71$ square feet.

Wilbur had planned to construct a five-foot wide wing using eighteen-foot long spars with two one-foot end caps, thereby achieving one hundred square feet per wing. He decided not to ship the long spars from Dayton, instead he would acquire them closer the assembly and test site. Later, on his way to Kitty Hawk, he was only able to find pine material in Norfolk sixteen feet long, so the spars were necessarily shorter, resulting in a wing of about seventeen and one-half feet.

Allowing for a one and one-half by five-foot section cut out of the lower surface for the pilot, Wilbur reported the area of the two wings totaled one hundred sixty-five square feet.[8] The weight estimate of one hundred ninety pounds held, thereby requiring a calculated wind velocity of about seventeen miles per hour to lift the craft with a pilot on board.

The value from Lilienthal's tables used to calculate the coefficient of lift had been based on a wing design with a camber of 1/12 shaped like a segment of a circle (see figure 3-3). The Wright's decided the change the shape with the intent of having better stability fore and aft. In their approach, the ribs in the wing "were of ash bent" to the shape shown in the figure following with a camber of about 1/23. There were no cross braces in the wing, as French sateen was put on with a bias (45-degrees) to provide the necessary rigidity.

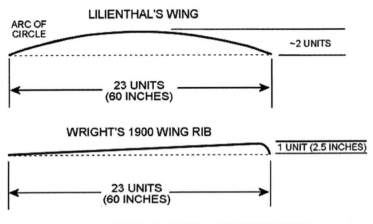

CAMBER OF WING EQUALS THICKNESS OVER WIDTH (CHORD)

Figure 3-3. Shown is the wing shape favored by Lilienthal with a camber of 1/12 along with the Wrights' design with a camber of about 1/23. The thinner approach did not improve the fore and aft or roll equilibrium as had been hoped, but did increase the aerodynamic efficiency of the wing.[9]

How the Pilot Maintained Control

It might have been easier at the onset to have the pilot sit upright on the wing with controls operated by his hands and feet. This created the problem of a larger cross-section to air, however, and required a stronger wind or ultimately a larger motor to stay airborne, so lying down was adopted. When landing it was planned the pilot would assume an upright posture, but gradually skidding across the sand in a prone position did not poise any particular hazard and was adopted as the preferred method.[10]

To control the fore and aft motion or roll of the glider, a moveable forward horizontal rudder was used (see figure 3-4). The pilot, prone on the lower wing, raised his body slightly to grab the two handles that controlled the position of the forward rudder. By pulling the handles up, the glider would descend and by pushing down, it would rise. A T-bar (not shown) was in the aft section and operated by the pilot's feet. Through cables it actuated the edges of the wing, providing lateral (roll) control of the glider.

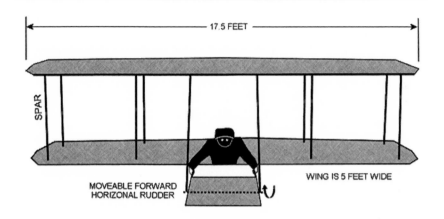

Figure 3-4. The Wrights' 1900 glider is flying toward the reader; the pilot is shown with his hands on the controls of the moveable forward horizontal rudder, providing pitch control. The pilot's feet rested on an aft T-bar, which controlled the wing twisting or warping for lateral or roll control. [Simplified illustration by the author based on a NASA simulation found at http://wright.nasa.gov/airplane/air1900.html; August 11, 2006.]

The reason for the forward horizontal rudder rather than placing it in the aft of the plane centered on safety, and was explained in a 1924 letter:

> We originally put the elevators in front at a negative angle to provide a system of inherent stability which it would have furnished had the center of pressure on the curved surfaces travelled forward, as was supposed, instead of backwards with increased angle of attack. We found that it produced inherent instability. We then tried using our 1900 glider backwards with the rear edge of the surfaces foremost, and found the stability much improved; but we retained the elevator in front for many years because it absolutely prevented a nose dive such as that in which Lilienthal and many others since have met their deaths.[11]

Off To Kitty Hawk

Having a design was the first step, but the glider had to be built and flown. The overriding requirement was to find a location where winds were fifteen to twenty miles per hour, relatively consistent and not filled with eddies that would be produced by land-based structures.

Not knowing what sections of the country might be suitable, Wilbur had written Octave Chanute on May 13, 1900 seeking his advice on a number of issues, including an appropriate test site. Among others, Chanute had suggested, "the Atlantic coast of South Carolina or Georgia" as the sand hills there were suitable places for learning how to fly a glider.

Drawn to the Atlantic coast, Wilbur wrote to the U.S. Weather Station at Kitty Hawk[12] on August 3, 1900 and obtained a response indicating favorable gliding conditions. Also, he received a letter from William J. Tate, local postmaster and Currituck County commissioner adding his own welcome, noting, "If you decide to try your machine here & come, I will take pleasure in doing all I can for your convenience & success & pleasure, & I assure you [–] you will find a hospitable people when you come among us."[13]

Kitty Hawk was it. Wilbur would buy, fabricate, and package most of the piece parts in Dayton for shipping to the Outer Banks along with his tools. He would acquire the wooden strips for the wing spars closer to Kitty Hawk and do the final assembly of his glider there. He finally confided his flying plans to his father, Milton, on September 3 writing:

> It is my belief that flight is possible, and, while I am taking up the investigation for pleasure rather than profit, I think there is a slight possibility of achieving fame and fortune from it. It is almost the only great problem which has not been pursued by a multitude of investigators, and therefore carried to a point where further progress is very difficult. I am certain I can reach a point much in advance of any previous workers in the field even if complete success is not attained just at present. At any rate, I shall have an outing of several weeks and see a part of the world I have never before visited.[14]

His sister, Katharine, also wrote Milton two day later noting, "we are in an uproar getting Will off. . . . If they can arrange it, Orv will go down as soon as Will gets the machine ready."[15]

Wilbur departed on September 6, taking a train from Dayton to Old Point Comfort, Virginia, a steamer to Norfolk, and a train to Elizabeth City, North Carolina (see figure 3-5). In a letter written to Milton on September 9 from Elizabeth City, Wilbur outlined the reasons for selecting the Outer Banks for his glider experiments:

I chose Kitty Hawk because it seemed the place which most closely met the required conditions. In order to attain support from the air it is necessary, with wings of reasonable size, to move through it at the rate of fifteen or twenty miles per hour. . . . It is safer to practice in a wind provided this is not too much broken up into eddies and sudden gusts by hills, trees etc. At Kitty Hawk which is on the narrow bar separating the Sound from the Ocean there are neither hills nor trees so that it offers a safe place for practice.

He continued in the letter to assure his father he would be careful, noting, "I have no intention of risking injury to any great extent, I will be careful, and will not attempt new experiments in dangerous situations. I think the danger much less than in most athletic games."[16]

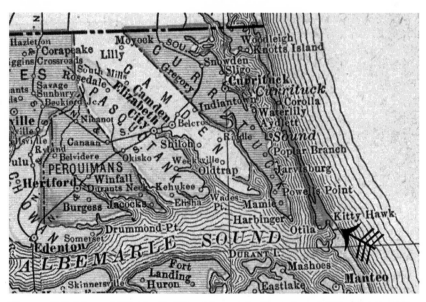

Figure 3-5. Map of Elizabeth City, Albemarle Sound and Kitty Hawk at the very end of Currituck County is depicted. [From *The New Ideal State and County Survey and Atlas of Pennsylvania* (Chicago: Rand, McNally & Co., 1911), page 72.]

His trip on a small boat from Elizabeth City down the Pasquotank River and through Albemarle Sound to Kitty Hawk was probably more dangerous than anything he would encounter flying that season, but he arrived safely the evening of September 12.

The next morning he found his way to the Tate's home where he received a warm welcome and made arrangements to room and board with them for the short term (see figure 3-6).

Figure 3-6. William Tate and his family initially hosted Wilbur Wright at Kitty Hawk while he constructed the glider. Wilbur wrote Milton, "His home is a two story frame with unplaned siding not painted, no plaster on the walls, which are ceiled with pine not varnished. He has no carpets at all, very little furniture, no books or pictures. . . . They are friendly and neighborly and [I] think there is rarely any real suffering among them."[17] [Wright photograph from the Library of Congress, touched up by the author.]

Building the Glider

Over the next two weeks Wilbur unpacked the prefabricated parts he had brought from Dayton and began assembling the glider in the front yard of the Tates. Mrs. Tate loaned him a sewing machine to rework the pre-sewn fabric wing panels, which were cut down to match the shorter wooden strips (wing spars), the only ones he could find in Norfolk enroute to Kitty Hawk.

On September 23, he wrote Milton stating his progress and outlining what he planned to accomplish during the forthcoming glider tests. Wilbur had not lost sight of how to logically proceed to achieve heavier-than-air powered fight. He would first learn how to control the machine then install a motor:

> I have my machine nearly finished. It is not to have a motor and is not expected to fly in the true sense of the word. My idea is merely to experiment and practice with a view to solving the problem of equilibrium.

Continuing, he reassured his father he did not plan to take any unnecessary risks providing the sound argument that an injury would curtail his experiments, something he did not want to happen:

> In my experiments I do not to expect to rise many feet from the ground, and in case I am upset there is nothing but soft sand to strike on. I do not intend to take dangerous chances, both because I have no wish to get hurt and because a fall would stop my experimenting, which I would not like at all. The man who wishes to keep at the problem long enough to really learn something positively must not take dangerous risks. Carelessness and overconfidence are usually more dangerous than deliberately accepted risks.[18]

Testing and Retesting

Orville arrived on September 28 and the two of them had the glider ready to fly by early October. It is likely that the first test occurred on October 3, as the reported wind that day seemed favorable. After several flights of the glider by itself, Wilbur climbed aboard as Orville and Bill Tate let out lines attached to either side of the machine. The craft rose into the air, but Wilbur was unable to control the stability fore and aft (pitch) and shouted, "Let me down!" He later explained he had promised his father not to take any unnecessary chances.

On October 8 and 9 the wind was "blowing 36 miles per hour" so no tests were made. On the 10th, however, with wind up to thirty miles per hour, Orville reported the machine was flown like a kite by "running down a number of strings to work the steering apparatus. The machine seemed a rather docile thing, and we taught it to behave fairly well."[19]

Less encouraging results were obtained by gliding at Look Out Hill just south of their camp. There a derrick was erected over which their rope was hoisted to put the glider into the air. Orville recounts the test:

> we sent it up about 20 feet, at which height we attempt to keep it by the manipulation of the strings to the rudder. The greatest difficulty is in keeping it down. It naturally wants to go higher & higher. When it begins to get too high we give it a pretty strong pull on the ducking string, to which it responds by making a terrific dart for the ground. If nothing is broken we start it up again. This is all practice in the control of the machine. When it comes down we just lay it flat on the ground and the pressure of the wind on the upper surface holds it down so tightly that you can hardly raise it again.
>
> After an hour or so of practice in steering, we laid it down on the ground to change some of the adjustments of the ropes, when without a sixteenth of a second's notice, the wind caught under one corner, and quicker than thought, it landed 20 feet away.[20]

The glider was severely damaged and at first the brothers even considered packing up and going home. By the next morning, however, things looked a bit brighter and they began the task of repair, which was accomplished in three days.

Figure 3-7. The unmanned glider is shown flying over the sands at Kitty Hawk in the fall of 1900. [Wright photograph from the Library of Congress.]

In a letter from Orville to Katharine on October 18, he reported that day they had taken the machine a mile below camp to try gliding on some steep hills. They had planned to have a pilot onboard but:

> The wind died out before we got there so all our experiments had to be made with the machine alone – no one on it. We let it up about four or five feet from the brow of the hill and then started it forward over the embankment. We were greatly pleased with the results excepting a few little accidents to the machine. It would glide out over the side at a height of 15 or twenty feet for about 30 feet, gaining, we think, in altitude all the while. After going about 30 feet out, it would sometimes turn up a little too much in front, when it would start back, increasing in speed as it came, and whack the side of the hill with terrific force. The result generally was a broken limb somewhere, but we hastily splint the breaks and go ahead. If the wind is strong enough and comes from the northeast, we will probably go down to Kill Devil Hills tomorrow, where we will try gliding on the machine.[21]

The following day they traveled three miles from their camp and spent the day gliding at Kill Devil Hills. In a letter to Octave Chanute on November 16, 1900, after Wilbur had returned to Dayton, he provided:

> After we found the difficulty of simultaneously maintaining both fore-and-aft and lateral balance we almost gave up the idea of attempting to glide, but just before returning we went down to the big hill which was about three miles from our camp and spent a day in gliding. Our plan of operation was for the aeronaut to lie down on the lower plane while two assistants grasped the ends of the [wings of the] machine and ran forward till the machine was supported on the air. The fore-and-aft equilibrium was in entire control of the rider, but the assistants ran beside the machine and pressed down the end which attempted to rise. We soon found that the machine could soar on a less angle than one in six and that if the machine was kept close to the slope (which was one in six by measurement) the speed rapidly increased till the runners could no longer keep up. The man on the machine then brought the machine slowly to the ground, so slowly in fact that the marks of the machine could be seen for twenty or thirty feet back from the point where it finally stopped.[22]

This gliding experience (see figure 3-7) was one of the most encouraging aspects of their trip to Kitty Hawk. It provided confidence in the fore and aft control, although it had not been possible to simultaneously operate the lateral wing warping at the same time.

Figure 3-7. Technique used to launch the glider down one of the Kill Devil Hills to test the handling of the aircraft. This photograph was taken of the 1902 glider. [Wright photograph, from the Library of Congress, cropped and enhanced by the author.]

Lessons Learned

One of the most puzzling conclusions drawn was the requirement of twenty-two miles per hour wind to sustain the flyer with an operator aboard. The original design called for a wing surface area of two hundred square feet, which, according to calculations, would have supported the craft and operator at fifteen miles per hour. With shortened wings, the wind speed had to be recalculated for a wing surface area of one hundred sixty-five, but this only increased the required wind velocity to about seventeen. Twenty-two miles per hour represented a twenty-nine percent increase, something that could not be explained. It was suspected the Wrights' wing camber of 1/23 versus the Lilienthal data that had assumed 1/12 was a contributing factor, but Wilbur was not sure.

Wilbur also noted, "We soon found that our arrangement for working the front rudder and twisting the planes [wings] were such that it was very difficult to operate them simultaneously."[23] Once this design defect was discovered, one or the other control was "tied off" for testing, since the materials to correct the problem were not available at Kitty Hawk.

On the positive side the drift, or drag as it is called today, was less than expected. In a twenty mile per hour wind, Wilbur had recorded in his notebook:

Weight Lifted (lbs)	Drift (lbs)
52	8 to 9
76	12
100	16
125	21

These values were much less than another experimenter had reported and portended well for the time when an engine would be installed on the flying machine.

Back to Dayton

On Saturday, October 13, Wilbur wrote Katharine from Elizabeth City starting the letter rather playfully, "Dear Stuckens: We have said 'Good bye Kitty, Good bye Hawk, good bye Kitty Hawk, we're gwine to leave you now.'"[24] He and Orville were headed for Norfolk the following morning and planned a stopover at Newport News to visit the shipyards. They anticipated arriving Dayton Saturday night, October 20, and Wilbur suggested porterhouse steaks for the Sunday meal.

On November 16, Wilbur resumed his correspondence with Chanute. He wrote a very long letter summarizing the results of the experiments at Kitty Hawk that began in mid-September and ended mid-October, a period of about four weeks. He described: the location; design, size and construction of the machine; methods of lateral and fore and aft stabilization; kiting and gliding trials; and some of the results and conclusions.

About one week later on November 23, Chanute responded with a brief note of congratulations on "your success in diminishing the resistance of the framing and demonstrating that the horizontal position for the operator is not as unsafe as I believed."[25] There was an astonishingly lack of comment on the fundamentals tested by the Wrights of control in the lateral and fore and aft planes.

Wilbur had thought through two of the aircraft's axes of instability, designed solutions, independently tested the results, and Chanute's interest was not even piqued! At this point Wilbur was thinking in four dimensions, three associated with the airframe and the fourth, time, as the center of pressure moved across the wings as a function of the angle of attack.

> *All mechanical design engineers who are worth their salt, think in three dimensions – the really good ones think in four.*

In Chanute's earth-bound mind, where structures such as railroad tracks, bridges, and stockyards were firmly attached to terra firma; this kind of airborne four-dimensional thinking was simply not in his cognitive structure. As Crouch would kindly note about Chanute's background: "It was not the sort of work that prepared a man to solve the problems of controlling a machine balanced on the head of a pin in the sky."[26]

Nevertheless, his correspondence, friendship, and support was important, as it provided Wilbur several things: (1) letter writing to Chanute forced him to distill, clarify and crystallize the tests, the results, and the conclusions; (2) on some practical issues such as availability of test equipment and discussion of some engineering matters, he would be of help; (3) access to information in previous flying experiments could prove to be valuable; and (4) Chanute provided encouragement at critical times to keep the Wrights motivated – a silent but effective cheerleader.

At that moment, however, Chanute was preparing an article on flying for *Cassier's Magazine*, and his mind was preoccupied. The Wrights has their own challenges and were already thinking about their next glider.

On the left is Wilbur, age 38, with Orville, age 34, shown on the right. [From the Library of Congress.]

---

[1] Orville and Wilbur Wright, "The Wright Brothers' Aeörplane," *The Century Magazine* (September 1908) 76:642.

[2] George Kibbe Turner, "The Men Who Learned To Fly," *McClures Magazine* (February 1908), p. 445.

[3] Wright, "Wright Brothers' Aeörplane," pp. 642–643

[4] This was determined in a test at Kitty Hawk in 1990. See Marvin W. McFarland, ed., *The Papers of Wilbur and Orville Wright* (1953, reprint; New York: McGraw Hill, 2001), p. 41.

[5] Wright, "Wright Brothers' Aeörplane," p. 643

[6] Ibid., p. 643. Inert is an interesting word to convey the meaning of being least perturbed by air transients.

[7] At this point the Wrights did not have direct access to Lilienthal's work, but used a reprint of his table found in *The Aeronautical Annual* of 1897. See McFarland, *Papers*, p. 42, n. 8.

[8] Ibid. p. 41. This corresponds to a calculated surface area of 5 x 17.5 x 2 – (1.5 x 5) = 167.5 ft^2, almost the same 165 reported by Wilbur who used 17 for the wings.

[9] Ibid., p. 43, n. 8 continued from previous page.

[10] Ibid., p. 43.

[11] Ibid., p. 44, n. 1.

[12] According to Catherine Albertson, *Legends of The Dunes of Dare* (Raleigh, NC: Capitol Printing Co., 1936), page 10, one legend for the name Kitty Hawk derives from the mosquito hawk, which became known as "skeeter hawk" and finally Kitty Hawk.

[13] See: http://memory.loc.gov/master/mss/mwright/03/03225/0002.jpg, July 16, 2006, Letter of August 18, 1900.

[14] See: http://memory.loc.gov/cgi-bin/ampage?collId=mwright&fileName=02/02055/mwright02055.db&recNum=0&itemLink=D?wright:55:./temp/~ammem_sfEj:: ;Letter of September 3, 1900; September 10, 2006.

[15] McFarland, *Papers*, p. 23.

[16] See: http://memory.loc.gov/master/mss/mwright/02/02055/0002d.jpg; Letter of September 9, 1900; July 17, 2006.

[17] See: http://memory.loc.gov/master/mss/mwright/02/02055/0004d.jpg; letter of September 23, 1900; July 17, 2006.

[18] Ibid.

[19] McFarland, *Papers*, p. 29.

[20] Ibid., p. 30.

[21] Ibid., pp. 38–39.

[22] Ibid., p. 43.

[23] Ibid. p. 41.

[24] See: http://memory.loc.gov/master/mss/mwright/02/02055/0006d.jpg; letter of October 13, 1900; July 17, 2006. This appears to be a parody on the traditional lyrics: good night ladies, good night ladies, good night ladies, we're gwine [going] to leave you now.

[25] McFarland, *Papers*, p. 44.

[26] Crouch, *The Bishop's Boys*, pp. 200–201.

Chapter 4

Jan-Aug 1901 – Larger Glider and Disappointments

Heavier-than-air flying machines are impossible.
— Lord Kelvin, 1895

Not within a thousand years would man ever fly!
— Wilbur Wright, 1901

When the Wrights left their glider in a sand holler at Kitty Hawk in October 1900, they departed for Dayton with no regrets. It had served them well and would later benefit Mrs. Tate, who would salvage the French sateen from the wings to sew dresses for her two daughters. Upon returning in July 1901, a storm the previous day, one of the worst ever, had relegated the skeletal remains to Davy Jones' sand locker. They were, however, focused on the future, not the past.

Probably some time before Wilbur left Kitty Hawk in late 1900, he had already started planning in his mind's eye the next glider. The problems encountered in the first model were indelibly imprinted in his brain as engineers learn through failures – something that has always been true. He and Orville had learned a number of things that did not work and each would be studied, analyzed and new approaches tried.

> *All progress begins in the mind's eye with the formulation of an idea that takes shape as obstacles are encountered, analyzed and overcome.*[1]

There was the difficulty or impracticality of simultaneously controlling both the lateral (roll) and fore and aft (pitch) controls of the machine. The lifting capacity had been less than predicted – was it the camber or something else? In any case, these issues had to be addressed and resolved before heavier-than-air flight was possible.

Achieving More Lift

Wilbur decided to use a more conservative value for the coefficient of lift. For the 1900 glider, he had selected an angle of attack of ten degrees, but now would use three degrees yielding the lower value for C_L of 0.54 versus the previous number of 0.825. Based on Kitty Hawk testing, he decided to use seventeen miles per hour for the wind velocity as opposed to the fifteen used for the 1900 design. He knew the machine would be larger and estimated a weight of one hundred pounds plus the operator for a total of two hundred forty pounds. From chapter 2, the equation for lift used by the Wrights to determine the wing surface area was:

$$L = S \times V^2 \times C_L \times k$$

Therefore: $240 = S \times (17)^2 \times 0.545 \times 0.005$

Solving the equation: $S = 240 / (289 \times 0.545 \times 0.005)$

Hence $S = 305$ square feet.

Each wing would be twenty-two feet long and seven feet wide, requiring twenty-foot long spars with one-foot end caps. This would have produced about three hundred eighty square feet, but the rear edges of the wing were gradually tapered (see figure 4-1); also subtracting from this was the portion lost in the pilot's location. Making these adjustments, the Wrights determined the wing lifting area to be two hundred ninety square feet.

The ribs were on one-foot centers and were bent to initially achieve a camber of about 1/12 versus the 1/23 used in the earlier model. It was hoped this would improve the lift to the value predicted by the Lilienthal tables.

Lateral Control

Using the foot-operated T-bar to twist the wings for lateral or roll control had not worked well. Unless the body of the operator were strapped to the frame of the aircraft, it was very difficult for either foot to apply pressure without a corresponding slippage of position. It was decided to attach the wing twisting or warping cables to a cradle, into which the operator's hips would be fitted. If the left wing dipped, the pilot would move his hips to the right initiating a correction.[2] Because of gravity, it might have been physically easier to move his hips in the same direction of the wing tilt, but this would have not been as intuitive, a safety factor critical in flying.

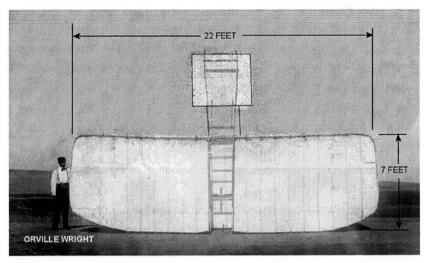

Figure 4-1. Orville Wright stands to the left of the top of the 1901 glider during an absence of wind in Kitty Hawk. Twenty-one ribs on one-foot centers are attached to the twenty-foot long wing spars. [Photograph by the Wrights from the Library of Congress, cropped, cleaned up and annotated by the author, 2006.]

Early Start to Kitty Hawk

When Wilbur began his aircraft experiments, he reported to Chanute they would be limited to the fall of the year so they didn't interfere with their normal bicycle business. By mid-1901, however, he had been bitten by the flying bug, and wanted to try out his new machine in Kitty Hawk.

An old friend, Charles Taylor, who agreed to work for the Wrights and run the shop in their absence, made this possible. On June 19, 1901 Wilbur wrote Chanute:

> Owing to changes in our business arrangements we shall start on our trip much earlier than we had expected, probably not later then July 10th, if we can get the material for our machine ready by that time. If this change should conflict with any plans of your own for use of the anemometer,

which you so kindly offered to let us have, please do not inconvenience yourself to oblige us. We can, if necessary, do without it.[3]

Chanute (below) had been corresponding with Wilbur since May 17, 1900 when he responded to the Wrights' first inquiry. Since this time he had gained a personal respect for Wilbur as being seriously interested in gliding and capable of producing some results that might lead to heavier-than-air flight. As a recognized aviation

expert, he wanted to stay current with on-going progress and had the sense the Wright brothers could possibly make a difference.

As Wilbur was forgoing his bread-and-butter business to leave early to test a new glider, some sort of breakthrough might have been in the wind. Chanute had never taken a first-hand assessment of the Wrights and decided it would be worthwhile to do so before they departed for the East Coast.

He had previously suggested to them a stopover in Dayton on an impending trip east, and now there wasn't much time to make it happen. On June 22 he wrote, "I will endeavor, within a very few days, to bring you the French anemometer." He was in Dayton on Wednesday, June 26 and spent the evening with the Wrights.

No record exists of the meeting, but it is likely Wilbur mentioned two forthcoming articles he was publishing on the angle of attack and the practicality of landing a glider with the operator in a horizontal position. As Chanute would later suggest in a June 28 letter – that glider associate Edward C. Huffaker, and corresponding aviation enthusiast, Dr. George A. Spratt, join the Wrights in Kitty Hawk to assist them at his expense – it is likely this possibility was broached that evening.

Somewhat reluctantly the Wrights would later accept the invitation for help and learned via another letter of July 3 that Chanute himself would accept their invitation to visit them in Kitty Hawk; he inquired as to the best time.

The Wrights arrived on the barrier island July 11, several days later than expected, delayed by "the greatest storm in the history of the place." They first erected a wooden building with prop-up garage-type doors on either end. It was large enough to house the glider, which was constructed inside and they had the machine completed by July 26.

Huffaker had arrived on the July 18, and Spratt on July 25. Chanute would not show up until the evening of August 4. The completed workshop with the glider removed is shown in figure 4-2.

Figure 4-2. Shown inside the Wrights' Kitty Hawk workshop, left to right, are Octave Chanute, Orville Wright, and Edward Huffaker, all seated, with Wilbur Wright, standing. Note the sleeping tent to the left with the water pump in front. [Wright photograph from the Library of Congress.]

Testing Reveals a Stability Problem

Orville, in a letter to Katharine on July 28, reports testing results to his younger sister in Dayton:

> Our first experiments were rather disappointing. The machine refused to act like our machine of last year and at times seemed to be entirely out of control. On occasion it began gliding off higher and higher (Will doing the gliding) until it finally came at a stop at a height variously estimated by Mr. Spratt and Huffaker at from 18 ft. to forty feet. This wound up in the most

encouraging performance of the whole afternoon. This was the very fix Lilienthal got into when he was killed. His machine dropped head first to the ground and his neck was broken. Our machine made a flat descent to the ground with no injury to the operator or machine. On another occasion the machine made another similar performance and showed that in this respect it is entirely safe. These were the first descents ever made after getting into the above-mentioned predicament.[4]

To improve the fore and aft or pitch handing of the machine, Wilbur first tried to reduce the size of the forward rudder to ten square feet, but as he noted in his diary, "on trial [there was] no particular improvement in control."

He determined the wing camber to be 1/12 when loaded with the pilot, and 1/17 when flown as a kite. The ribs tended to flatten out under load, something he would have liked to avoid. These curvatures were greater than the 1900 glider of 1/23, and he suspected at low angles of attack, the center of pressure did not stay forward of the center of gravity, as in the old machine, but quickly reversed producing the instability.

Lilienthal had warned of this effect with curvatures of 1/8, but Wilbur had taken precaution by modifying the shape of the rib producing most of the curvature on the leading edge, something he believed potentially mitigated this problem. But before modifying the camber, he decided to run a test on a single wing to prove or disprove the suspicion.

In a subsequent paper delivered to a group of engineers in Chicago in the fall of 1901, he presented a graphic (see figure 4-3) and described the tests.

At an angle of attack of approximately twelve degrees shown in the top illustration, a relatively low air velocity (note size of air arrow) will support the wing, producing a center of pressure in front of the center of gravity. This causes the wing to rise, unless held down by the force shown as the dashed arrow, which in the case of the glider was a rope. This was the reason the piloted glider had a tendency to glide "off higher and higher."

Reducing the angle of attack to about four degrees and increasing the velocity of the air caused the center of gravity and air pressure to coincide and the only small stabilizing force required was the so-called drag or drift of the wing. This is shown as the small horizontal dashed arrow to the left on the center illustration.

With high-velocity airflow and a small angle of attack, the center of pressure, rather than staying ahead of the center of gravity, as anticipated by Wilbur, actually moved back. Since there is no practical way to produce the force to hold up the leading edge, the wing would lose lift (stall) and dive to the ground. When this occurred with Wilbur piloting the glider, the forward horizontal rudder prevented a nosedive and saved him for another day of testing.

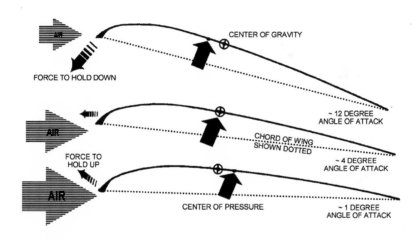

Figure 4-3. The three cross-sections of the wings at different angles of attack are reproduced from the lantern slide Wilbur used in his address to a group of engineers in the fall of 1901. The different-sized arrows marked "AIR" represent varying degrees of velocity. Their resultants are the solid black arrow labeled "Center of Pressure" that produces an upward force on the wing at different angles of attack. [Illustration by the author, 2006.]

In his address, Wilbur reported, "It at once occurred to me that here was the answer to our problem . . . This point having been definitely settled, we proceeded to truss down the ribs of the whole machine, so as to reduce the depth of curvature."[5]

The trussing down was accomplished by placing a third spar on the top center of each rib and running a wire from one end of the rib to the other. Pulling the wire taught forced the rib down, reducing the curvature (see figure 4-4).[6]

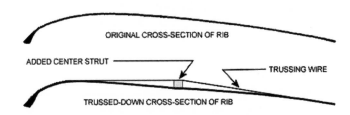

Figure 4-4. Shown on the top is the original rib cross-section and below the technique used by Wilbur to reduce the camber of all the ribs used in the wing.[7] [Illustration by the author, 2006.]

This solved the instability problem, leading Wilbur to report to the engineers:

> On resuming our gliding, we found that the old conditions of the preceding year had returned; and after a few trials, made a glide of 366 feet and soon one after of 389 feet. The machine with its new curvature never failed to respond promptly to even small movements of the [forward] rudder. The operator could cause it to almost skim the ground, following the undulation of its surface, or he could cause it to sail out almost on the level with the starting point, and passing high above the foot of the hill, gradually settle down to the ground.[8]

It is worthwhile noting that when the fore and aft (pitch) instability problem arose, both Huffaker and Spratt had also suggested it was caused by a reversal of pressure at low angles of attack. This was Wilbur's instinct as well, but he noted, "instead of using the arc of a circle [like Lilienthal], we had made the curve of the machine very abrupt at the front, so as to expose the least possible area to this downward pressure." Therefore, he wasn't sure and decided to run a test to gather data.

> *The measure of a good engineer is: to gather relevant data, carefully analyze the data and test conditions, and judiciously modify the design.*

Testing Identifies High Drag

In Wilbur's diary of Tuesday, July 30, 1901 he recorded as problem number three:

> 3. The resistance of the framing seems to be larger than we expected, being in fact nearly double. We attribute this to the incomplete finish of some of the details but especially to a position of the cutting edge of the framing caused by straightening out of the longitudinal ribs, thus presenting surface of $1^3/_4$ inches broad at an angle of about 60°. We decided to return to last year's construction.[9]

When the ribs were trussed down to decrease the camber, this caused the leading edge of the wings to rotate slightly upward, providing a larger cross-section to the wind than desired. This was corrected by using the same construction technique that had been employed on the 1900 glider (see figure 4-5).

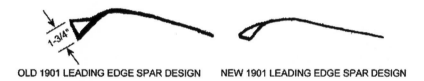

OLD 1901 LEADING EDGE SPAR DESIGN   NEW 1901 LEADING EDGE SPAR DESIGN

Figure 4-5. Two sketches from Wilbur's logbook are shown. On the left is the old large undesirable leading edge cross-section that produced a large drag, and on the right, the new design taken from the 1900 machine. [McFarland, *Papers*, page 78, annotated by the author, 2006.]

It is not clear why the design was changed from the 1900 model, but it may have been to produce a more robust leading edge spar, which would be less prone to damage on hard landings. One of the positive test results recorded in Wilbur's July 30 diary entry was, "1. The machine is strong. It has suffered no injury although severely used in some forty landings."[10]

The design modification proved to be effective. Wilbur's diary entry of August 7, 1901 confirms the efficacy of the change, as he records, "Found drift or head resistance of framing reduced some three pounds as a result of changes."[11]

There were also other positive results coming out of the experiments. The three-hundred-square-foot machine had been tested in winds as high as eighteen miles per hour and was manageable. "The lateral [roll] balance of the machine seems all that could be desired," reported Wilbur.[12] A test flight is shown in figure 4-6.

Figure 4-6. Wilbur is shown flying the 1901 glider with both hands holding the forward horizontal rudder. The center spar used in trussing down the lower wing ribs can be clearly seen. [Wright photograph from the Library of Congress, cleaned up and enhanced by the author, 2006.]

Lingering Unanswered Problems

Still, there persisted a significant problem with inadequate lift that had also been discovered in the earlier model. "The lift is not much over 1/3 that indicated by the Lilienthal tables," Wilbur lamented and that dashed "our hopes of obtaining actual practice in the air . . . to about one fifth of what we hoped."[13]

But the most depressing result had to do with turning the glider: "we proved that our machine does not turn (*i.e.* circle) towards the lowest wing under all circumstances," Wilbur reported in a letter to Chanute, "a very unlooked for result and one which completely upsets our theories as to the causes which produce the turning to the right or left."[14]

Wilbur had carefully observed birds, which turned left or right by raising the opposite wing. Wing twisting or warping provided exactly the same action but the machine would not turn, as it would slide or slip in the direction of the raised wing, a result that was not totally understood. Wilbur had not yet come to grips with the third axis of control of an aircraft, yaw, and would find this the most difficult to conquer.

The train ride home was not exuberant as it had been the previous year, and Orville recalled his brother remarking, "Not within a thousand years would man ever fly!"[15]

Kill Devil Hill where the Wrights conducted glider tests. [Photograph by the Wrights from the Library of Congress, enhanced by the author, 2006.]

---

[1] The author is indebted to Eugene S. Ferguson author of *Engineering and the Mind's Eye* for the mind's eye concept.

[2] Marvin W. McFarland, ed., *The Papers of Wilbur and Orville Wright* (1952, reprint; New York: McGraw-Hill, 2001), p. 81.

[3] Ibid., p. 55.

[4] Ibid., p. 75.

[5] Ibid., p. 111.`

[6] Although not mentioned by Wilbur, the design approached created a pre-stressed rib, which was much less likely to change shape with loading.

[7] It was not apparent from the reproduced trussing-down sketch on page 81 from McFarland's *Papers* as to how Wilbur accomplished the task. The author sketched out his approach and later was comforted to find in the Library of Congress online Wright papers, the same approach.

[8] McFarland, *Papers*, p. 111.

[9] Ibid., p. 78.

[10] Ibid.

[11] Ibid., p. 79.

[12] Ibid., p. 78.

[13] Ibid., p. 77.

[14] Ibid., p. 84.

[15] This is the version of the quote provided by Fred C. Kelly, *The Wright Brothers: A Biography Authorized by Orville Wright* (New York: Harcourt, Brace & Co., 1943), p. 72. This variation has the most drama. Wilbur, in an after-dinner speech (see Fred Howard, *Wilbur and Orville Wright: A Biography of the Wright Brothers* (Mineola, NY: Dover Publications, 1987/1998), page 67, provided another version, "I must confess that, in 1901, I said to my brother Orville that man would not fly for fifty years."

Chapter 5

Aug-Dec 1901 – Wind Tunnel Testing

Back to basics or back to first principles. (The last hope of a frustrated engineer where everything else has failed.)

– Anonymous

Katharine wrote to her father, Milton, on Monday, August 26, 1901 reporting, "The boys walked in unexpectedly on [last] Thursday morning. . . . [They] haven't had much to say about flying. They can only talk about how disagreeable Huffaker was. Mr. Chanute was there for a week. Will is sick with a cold or he would have written to you before this."[1]

A dejected and travel-weary Wilbur, ill with a cold, was not immediately ready to focus on the problems they experienced with the glider at Kitty Hawk. In a few days, however, he began to summarize the trials and compiled the results in a lengthy letter to Chanute dated August 29. On the same day from Chicago, Chanute wrote a letter to Wilbur with an invitation:

> I have been talking with some of the members of the Western Society of Engineers. The conclusion is that the members would be very glad to have an address, or a lecture from you, on your gliding experiments. We have a meeting on the 18th of September, and can set that for your talk. If you conclude to come [to Chicago] I hope you will do me the favor of stopping at my house. We should have the photos you want to use about a week before the lecture in order to get lantern slides. The more the better. Please advise me.[2]

Katharine would write her father on September 3 about Wilbur's speaking opportunity, stating somewhat braggingly, "Will was about to refuse but I nagged him into going. He will get acquainted with some scientific men and it may do him a lot of good." Wilbur's response to Chanute on the previous day simply said, "After your kindness in interesting yourself in obtaining an opportunity to address the society, for me, I hardly see how to refuse." The time was too short, he noted, for anything elaborate but as Chanute had suggested he would use pictures.

This was, in retrospect, a most fortuitous opportunity for the elder statesman to astutely place Wilbur in a spotlight. It provided the budding inventor a chance to step away from the trees again, as when he started the project, and examine the forest. Thus, he could more objectively and more clearly lay out what he and Orville were trying to accomplish, how they had proceeded, and the lessons learned. Addressing a group of Chicago engineers would propel Wilbur's thinking to a new level and in the process focus his agile mind on precisely what had to be done to be successful in achieving heavier-than-air flight.

Chanute would later advise him the engagement would be "Ladies' night," provided he had no objections. Most likely the wives of the engineers found little interest in subjects such as building a stockyard, laying a new rail line, or running a sewer pipe, so "Some Aeronautical Experiments" was a title most likely to pique their interest. Besides, their sharp elbows would keep the engineers awake once the lights were dimmed for the lantern slides after Wilbur's introductory remarks.

Summary of Remarks: Control, Control, Control

Wilbur's address to the Western Society of Engineers on September 18 began with a brief review of the difficulties, which "obstruct the pathway to success in flying." These fell into three classes: (1) lightweight airframe design, (2) lightweight powerful engines, and (3) airframe stability. He argued the first two were sufficiently advanced to pose no real problems, but the inability to balance and steer still confronted success. "When this one feature has been worked out the age of flying machines will have arrived, for all other difficulties are of minor importance."[3] Although some of his assertions about the ease the first two problems, particular the engine's propeller, would be quickly overcome were overoptimistic, his basic approach, nevertheless, was fundamentally sound.

Built-in Airframe *Control* – Controls managed by the pilot had always been their first mandatory step to successful flying. He spent a considerable amount of time technically explaining how they achieved fore and aft control (pitch) with the forward horizontal rudder, and lateral control (roll) with wing twisting in a manner akin to the birds. He contrasted their approach to that of Lilienthal, who shifted his body weight to achieve stability, something that proved to be inadequate. The controls had to be an integral part of the airframe structure and under the positive control of the pilot. This approach is what set him apart from other experimenters.

Pilot *Control* – Wilbur forthrightly asserted, "practice is the secret of flying." To explain, he chose an analogy of "learning to ride a fractious [unruly] horse." You can learn to ride by sitting on the fence and observing the beast, retire to a comfortable place and figure out how to overcome his jumps and kicks, or get on and take your lumps. While the former is safer, that possibility does not exist for the airplane, so you must climb aboard and take off.

Herein was a problem. The 1900 glider was too small to support a man's weight to learn to fly so the 1901 model was made considerably larger – from one hundred sixty-five to three hundred eight square feet. Still, there existed insufficient lift in winds of reasonable velocities to attain much piloting experience.

Wilbur believed the formula for calculating lift was substantially correct, but began to suspect the coefficients of lift found in the Lilienthal table were in error. To validate or disprove these, the Wright brothers had already begun to conduct experiments to compare their results with Lilienthal's and had discovered differences.

Airfoil Testing *Control* – This would become a major focus of the Wrights' work in the three months following the address to the engineers. It was only briefly mentioned by Wilbur that evening and subsequently he and Chanute would discuss how much of the testing techniques and results should be placed into the written transcript of the meeting. This unanticipated avenue of work had not occurred to the brothers when the airplane project was undertaken, but producing accurate airfoil data now clearly stood between them and success.

The Whirling Apparatus

After some preliminary airfoil testing on a moving bicycle, a wind tunnel sixteen inches square and six feet long was constructed (see figure 5-1). It produced air moving between twenty-five and thirty-five miles per hour from a two-blade belt-driven fan that was powered off a line-and-pulley shaft in the Wrights' workshop. A single-cylinder gasoline engine spun the overhead shaft, turning a drill press, lathe, band saw, and grinder. For wind tunnel testing, the fan was attached to one end of the shaft that spun a grinding wheel and the wooden frame was positioned so the air was directed into the end with the metal frame, called a cowling.

Figure 5-1. Shown is a replica of the 1901 wind tunnel constructed by the Wright brothers. [Photograph from a U.S. Government website, enhanced, annotated, and background removed by the author, 2006.]

In a letter to Chanute, Wilbur pointed out "The wind from the fan is rendered uniform in direction by the same means which Prof. Marey employed so successfully in the photographs you showed us at Kitty Hawk."[4] Marey had used silk gauze, but the Wrights adopted a wire mesh in conjunction with a pigeonhole-straightening device "made of sheet iron so as not to obstruct the flow of air." To observe what was happening in the wind tunnel, Wilbur wrote, "We have accordingly mounted the [pressure-measuring] instrument in a long box or trough, with a glass cover."[5]

The initial design approach of the instrument, however, limited its accuracy because of undesirable perturbations in the airflow, which introduced, according to Wilbur's estimate, errors "of perhaps ten percent." Nevertheless, based on measured results he reported to Chanute, "It would appear that Lilienthal is very much nearer the truth than we have heretofore been disposed to think."[6] He suspected the errors in wing lifting capacity were stemming from the coefficient of air pressure used by Lilienthal of $k = 0.005$, now believing the correct value should be 0.0033.

To produce more accurate results, the Wrights designed a new pressure-measuring device. It was described to Chanute as, "The essential principle of it is the use of a *normal* plane in measuring the pressure on an *inclined* surface. And as both are acted upon simultaneously by the wind, a change in velocity, with its resulting change in pressure, does not cause oscillations"[7] in the measurements.

If this sounds complicated, don't dismay. Even Chanute, who had an accompanying sketch from Wilbur and a more complete textural description, did not understand it and would ask for a better explanation. The flow of wind tunnel air was not completely steady because of vibrations in the drive mechanisms. This caused air velocity pulsations and made accurate readings difficult. The Wrights designed what would be called today a differential system, whereby the pulsations could be effectively cancelled.

A photograph of the measuring device is shown in figure 5-2. The *normal* plane referred to above was comprised of the "four resistance planes" that totaled eight square inches. The *inclined* surface was attached to the upper part and identified as "airfoil under test." How it works is not immediately clear, therefore two follow-on illustrations have been prepared to explain its operation.

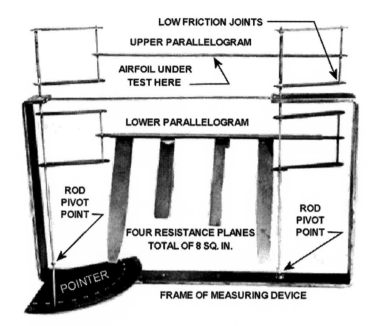

LOW FRICTION JOINTS

UPPER PARALLELOGRAM

AIRFOIL UNDER
TEST HERE

LOWER PARALLELOGRAM

ROD
PIVOT
POINT

ROD
PIVOT
POINT

FOUR RESISTANCE PLANES
TOTAL OF 8 SQ. IN.

POINTER

FRAME OF MEASURING DEVICE

Figure 5-2. Photograph of the Wrights lift balance used in wind tunnel testing to measure the effectiveness of different airfoils. [Photograph from U.S. Government website, enhanced and annotated by the author.]

Their innovative measuring approach employed the use of a pair of hinged rectangular frames, which are depicted in figure 5-3. In the upper illustration, air acting on the airfoil causes the moveable bar to rotate to the right. Notice this configuration maintains the same relative position of the airfoil with respect to the moving air. Aptly, such an arrangement is called a parallelogram. Unless a spring or other force restrains the moveable arm, it will simply move to the right, limited only by stops on the mechanical structure.

In the lower illustration, the arms are rotated about forty-five degrees to the right. The air moving across this arrangement acts on the "four resistance plates" below the moveable bar causing the arms to straighten out and move to the left.

Thus, there exist two opposing forces, both produced by the same flowing air. Hence, perturbations in the air produced equal and opposite effects, thereby yielding steady test results.

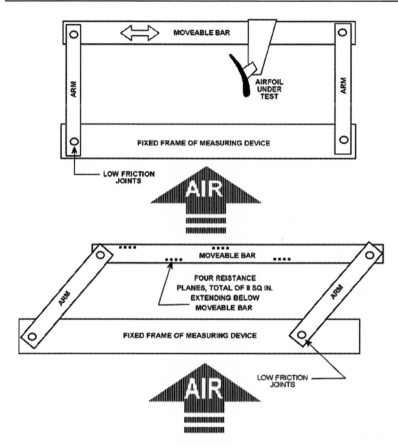

Figure 5-3. Top – Moving air caused the airfoil under test to rotate the arms to the right. Bottom – As air impacted the four resistance planes, the arms moved to the left. [Illustrations by the author, 2006.]

The Wrights, in their approach, combined two such parallelograms with one end of the arms attached to vertical rods that pivoted on a single supporting frame (see figures 5-2 and 5-4). A pointer and a protractor scale were added to measure the resulting angle, from which the lift could later be calculated.

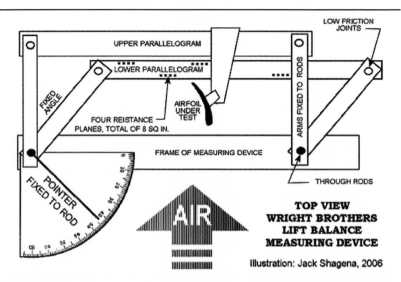

Figure 5-4. The top view of the Wrights' instrument to measure the lift of an airfoil is shown. It was called a *lift balance*, as the four resistance planes on the lower parallelogram were impacted by the same moving air and tended to "balance out" the airfoil movement, which was measured in degrees by the pointer on the protractor scale. [Illustration by the author, 2006.]

Testing Results

Another device for measuring drag was also constructed and after about two months they had gathered data on dozens of airfoils examining the aspect (length to width) of wings, different cambers, and variations in airfoil thicknesses. Wind tunnel testing had taken them back to basics or back to first principles, from which they were able to compile accurate lift and drag data. This was a critical step toward inventing the airplane, and using these data, a much-improved flyer would be built the following year.

[1] Marvin W. McFarland, ed., *The Papers of Wilbur and Orville Wright* (1953, reprint; New York: McGraw-Hill, 2001), p. 84.

[2] Ibid., p. 91

[3] All quotes in the section are taken for Wilbur's address to the Western Society of Engineers as found on pages 99 to 118 of McFarland, *Papers*.

[4] McFarland, *Papers*, p. 134.

[5] Ibid., pp 134–135.

[6] Ibid., p. 135.

[7] Ibid., p. 142.

Chapter 6

1902 – Glider and Confidence Grows

While lying awake last night, I studied out a new vertical rudder.

– Orville Wright, October 3, 1902

"The flying machine is in process of making now," reported Katharine to her dad on August 20, 1902. "Will spins the sewing machine around by the hour while Orv squats around marking the places to sew. There is no place in the house to live but I'll be lonesome enough by this time next week" after they leave for Kitty Hawk. She was concerned that both of them were "thin and nervous," but believed "they would be alright when they get down in the sand where the salt breezes blow."[1]

The Wrights arrived in Kitty Hawk on Thursday, August 28, having departed Dayton three days earlier. Mother Nature had inflicted some damage to the camp during their absence and Wilbur reported this to Chanute on Tuesday, September 2, 1902:

> During the year the winds blew all of the foundation, which consisted of sand, out from under the building and let the ends drop down two feet, thus giving the a shape of a dromedary's back. We were a little discouraged at first but after two days' work we raised it to its original level and put foundation post under it. We do not anticipate any further trouble from this source, and in putting up the addition will put in post to begin with. It will probably take the balance of this week to complete our building and some improvements. [2]

This year they were determined to have housing more suitable than the tent of the previous two years. Dan Tate helped them erect an addition to the existing building and by September 6 they were putting on finishing touches and moving in the kitchen. A photograph of the kitchen is shown in figure 6-1, and it is remarkably organized, providing a modicum of insight into the minds of engineers.

Figure 6-1. *A place for everything and everything in its place* is an apt description of the Wrights' neatly arranged kitchen. [Wright brothers photograph available from the Library of Congress.]

In a letter from Wilbur to George Spratt, who was uncertain as to being able to join the Wrights at Kitty Hawk, he promoted the improved living conditions hoping he would be enticed to come:

> Our kitchen is immensely improved, and then we have made beds on the second floor and now sleep aloft. We have put battens on the cracks [between the vertical board siding] of the whole building including the addition, so it is much tighter and waterproof than before as well as more sandproof. Our new well goes down six or eight feet below low water mark on the ocean (about ten feet deeper than last year) and we now have good water. We also have a bicycle which runs much better on the sand . . . other improvements too numerous to mention, and no Huffaker and no mosquitoes, so we are having a splendid time.[3]

Building a Grander Glider

With material shipped from Dayton to Kitty Hawk and some reclaimed parts obtained from disassembling the 1901 glider, the Wrights began construction of their new machine on September 8. To support the weight of the pilot, it would be larger than previous models, with a wingspan of thirty-two feet, one inch. Each wing was five feet wide and built with a shape, camber, and aspect ratio derived from wind tunnel testing to provide good lift and low drag or drift. It is instructive to compare glider specifications for the three models built – see table 6-1.

Table 6-1. Shown are the significant characteristics of the Wright gliders built in 1900, 1901 and 1902.

Glider Specifications	1900	1901	1902
Wing length (feet)	17.5	22	32.1
Wing width (feet)	5	7	5
Total wing area (sq. ft.)	165	290	305
Camber (approx.)	1/23	1/12-1/17	1/23
Aspect ratio	3.5	3.14	6.42
Tail	No	No	Yes
Weight (pounds)	50	100	116 ½

Compared to the 1900 model, the length of the wing had almost doubled, while the width remained the same, producing about a seventy-five percent more surface area.[4] For the new model, this yielded a length to width aspect ratio of 6.42, a desirable characteristic learned from wind tunnel testing. In the 1901 model they had experimented with a 1/12 to 1/17 camber, but also found through testing a more advantageous value to be 1/23 (like the 1900 glider). With the anticipation of solving the adverse yaw turning problem experienced in the 1901 glider, twin fixed vertical tails with a total surface area of about twelve square feet were installed on the new machine.

The 1902 machine was completed by September 19 and this year Orville would participate in glider piloting, and like Wilbur the previous year, had an accident. Both engineers, however, learned by mistakes and gradually gained proficiency at flying.

Testing, Modifications, and Retesting

Initial tests were rather encouraging as they found the machine would glide on a angle of seven degrees or less, and Orville recorded in his diary "we are convinced the trouble with the 1901 machine [adverse yaw] is overcome by the vertical tail."[5] A few days later, after many more test flights, a confident Wilbur wrote to Chanute on Tuesday, September 23:

> The action of the machine is almost perfect, or rather it controls both fore-and-aft [pitch] & transversely [laterally or roll]] just as we wish it to; and the capacity for control if properly utilized will meet any emergency, we think." The steering to right & left is now all right, the machine always turning towards the low wing. The efficiency of the machine is fully 3° better than last year.[6]

That day they had made seventy-five glides with "a usual length of 150 to 225 feet," lasting about ten to twelve seconds.

Figure 6-2. Flight of the 1902 glider with the twin fixed tails. [Wright brothers photograph from the Library of Congress, cropped and enhanced by the author.]

This confidence exuded by Orville and Wilbur stemmed from achieving more flight time than had been heretofore possible, and with their flying skills improving, they were becoming sell-assured and thought they could handle any instability that might occur. They were not aware that lingering in the shadows, however, was the yet unsolved adverse yaw problem.

During a test on September 30, their brother Lorin (right) arrived at the camp unexpectedly to assist Wilbur and Orville with

preparations for their experiments. In addition, Spratt arrived the following day also ready to help with flight testing.

An Engineering Breakthrough

Providing a rebuttal to a deposition in 1912, Wilbur recalled a very different view of the problem faced in 1902:

> The entire loss of control in these [1902 test] flights caused us a great deal of uneasiness, and the flights were almost suspended until some means could be devised so as to make the machine safe under all conditions of flight. . . . After a good deal of thought the idea occurred to us that by making the vane in the rear adjustable, so that it could be turned so as to entirely relieve the pressure on that side towards the low side of the machine, and to create a pressure on the side towards the high wing equal or greater than the differences in the resistance of the high and low wings.

The idea to make the tail moveable had come from Orville, when, on the morning of October 3, he announced to those assembled at the breakfast, "While lying awake last night, I studied out a new vertical rudder." He was not at all sure how his older brother, Wilbur, would respond to the idea but was delighted when he quickly adopted the suggestion and added an improvement of coupling the wing twisting controls to the vertical rudder, thereby relieving the pilot of the responsibility to remember to move both simultaneously (see figure 6-3).

At this moment the solution to controlling the yaw axis of flight was invented, and with it, the world's first almost practical heavier-than-air airplane was born.

Figure 6-3. The 1902 flying machine with the single moveable tail installed. [Wright brothers photograph from the Library of Congress, cropped and enhanced by the author.]

Chanute arrived on October 5 along with Augustus Herring, who had built a glider for the elder statesman, which was to be tested at the Wright camp. Several days later another glider built by Charles Lamson for Chanute arrived at Kitty Hawk, and over the next week and a half these machines would be evaluated with the help of the Wrights. Neither tested very well and a disappointed Chanute and Herring departed on October 14. Lorin had headed back to Dayton the previous day, leaving only the two Wright brothers and Spratt in the camp.

Testing of the Wrights' machine continued, and on Thursday, October 23, Orville writes to Katharine:

Everybody is out of the camp but Will and myself. Spratt left Monday. We had a good time [flying] last week after Chanute & Herring left. . . .

The past five days have been the most satisfactory for gliding that we have had. In two days we made over 250 glides, or more than we had made all together up to the time Lorin left. We have gained considerable proficiency in the handling of the machine now, so that we are able to take it out in any kind of weather.[7]

The brothers believed they had finally mastered flying, so after packing up their machine along with the two gliders that belonged to Chanute, the much-satisfied duo departed Tuesday morning October 28 for Dayton. It was, according to Wilbur, "a very exciting but tiresome trip."

Looking for an Engine

In early December Wilbur wrote to a number of manufacturers of gasoline engines seeking an eight to nine break horsepower engine weighing not more than one hundred eighty pounds. He would receive replies from ten companies, but none met the desired specifications.[8] If they required an engine meeting those numbers, they would have to build it themselves. Indeed, they were up to the task, with talented machinist Charles Taylor providing much of the effort.

Not apparent at this time, was the considerable difficulty of designing the propeller. It would provoke much passionate discussion between the brothers before a final engineering breakthrough would surface.

Sand crab found at Kitty Hawk. [Wright photograph from the Library of Congress.]

U.S. Life Saving Station at Kitty Hawk is shown with four of the crew. [Enhanced Wright photograph from the Library of Congress.]

---

[1] Marvin W. McFarland, ed., *The Papers of Wilbur and Orville Wright* (1953, reprint; New York: McGraw-Hill, 2001), p. 244.

[2] Ibid., p. 246.

[3] Ibid., p. 253.

[4] Orville, in a diary entry of September 19, states the total square footage to be 305 with the front rudder contributing 15. This leaves 290 for the wings.

[5] McFarland, *Papers*, p. 255.

[6] McFarland, *Papers*, p. 261. The three degrees improvement means gliding at an angle three degree less that the 1901 model.

[7] Ibid., pp. 279–280.

[8] Ibid., p. 287.

Chapter 7

1903 – Powered Flight Finally Achieved

Of all inventions, the alphabet and printing press excepted, those inventions which abridge distance have done the most for civilization.

– Thomas Babington McCaulay, 1849

In the beginning of 1903, the Wrights faced many challenges, several of them new. They would have to design and fabricate a lightweight gasoline engine, figure out how to construct an efficient propeller and drive chain, and design a much larger and heavier flying machine to carry the engine and fuel. As the ribs in the previous machine had a tendency to flatten out with load, thereby changing the flying characteristics, a sturdier rib would now be required. The 1902 glider had used the vertical struts from the machine of the previous year, but to reduce drag, new strut configurations would be tested in a wind tunnel to find more efficient leading and trailing edge designs. Also, with a larger glider it would be necessary to build a bigger construction shed at Kitty Hawk, and get the testing completed before cold weather set in.

And of course there was the bicycle business to keep running. Being hardworking and industrious, they would find a way to get everything done.

Power Plant

Recognizing that building a lightweight gasoline engine to power their new machine represented a difficult challenge, the design was already under way in late 1902. By February 12, the engine was running, but the next day gasoline inadvertently dripped on the engine causing the lubrication of a bearing to be washed away. After a short time the bearing overheated and froze to the shaft.[1] Energy stored in the momentum of the flywheel caused the aluminum casting to break and there was nothing to do but start over.

A new casting was ordered and arrived April 20. The engine was rebuilt and testing again resumed in May. Wilbur had described the motor to Spratt in a letter dated February 28:

> We recently built a four-cylinder gasoline engine with 4" piston and 4" stroke to see how powerful it would be, and what it would weigh. At 670 revolutions per min. it developed 8¼ horsepower, brake test. By speeding it up to 1,000 rev. we will easily get eleven horsepower and possibly a little more at still higher speed, though the increase is not in exact proportion to the increase in number of revolutions. The weight including the 30-pound flywheel is 140 lbs.[2]

More progress on the motor is found in a later letter to Spratt from Wilbur, this one dated June 28:

> Since putting in heavier springs to actuate the valves on our engine we have increased its power to nearly sixteen horsepower, and at the same time reduced the amount of gasoline consumed per hour to about one half of what it was before.[3]

Orville would later report that the sixteen horsepower would only last for a few seconds after starting, reducing to twelve after a run time of one minute.[4] Nevertheless, this was still good news, as initial objectives had been to achieve eight to nine horsepower with a weight not exceeding one hundred eighty pounds. Their engine could produce twelve horsepower and only weighed one hundred forty pounds. These results were obtained through good engineering, and the dedicated and skilful assistance of machinist, Charles E. Taylor.

Propeller Design

Initially, the Wrights believed a propeller design would not be difficult, as it was only necessary to analyze and modify work already done in the marine industry. An examination of extant literature revealed that the configurations of propellers used on steamships and other boats all had been developed empirically, that is, through trial and error processes. For them, the time was too short to guess – a more scientific approach would have to be undertaken. They later wrote about this decision:

As we were not in a position to undertake a long series of practical experiments to discover a propeller suitable for our machine, it seemed necessary to obtain such a thorough understanding of the theory of its reactions as [this] would enable us to design them from calculation alone.[5]

Developing a new theory would be very difficult, as Wilbur wrote to Spratt in December 1902, "We have recently done a little experimenting with screws and are trying to get a clear understanding of just how they work and why. It is a very perplexing problem. . . ."[6] Indeed, it was an intellectual challenge full of confusing conditions. Looking back in 1909, they summarized it this way:

What at first seemed a simple problem became more complex the longer we studied it. With the machine moving forward, the air flying backward, the propeller turning sideways, and nothing standing still, it seemed impossible to find a starting point from which to trace the various simultaneous reactions. Contemplation of it was confusing. After long arguments, we often found ourselves in the ludicrous position of having been converted to the other's side, with no more agreement than when the discussion began.[7]

A breakthrough came, however, when they decided to treat the propeller as a rotary wing. At first impression such an approach might seem a bit bizarre, but the Wrights astutely noted, "It was apparent that a propeller was simply an aeroplane [*i.e.* wing] travelling in a spiral course. As we could calculate the effect of a aeroplane [wing] travelling in a straight course, why should we not be able to calculate the effect on one traveling in a spiral course?"[8]

It is easier to comprehend that a propeller is a rotary wing by recognizing this is the way a helicopter flies, and they are sometimes referred to as rotary-wing aircraft. A tuning propeller meets the air at an angle of attack analogous to the wing of an aircraft as can be seen in figure 7-1. This is not immediately understood from the side view of the propeller on the left, but when it has been rotated ninety degrees, the end of the blade is clearly seen attacking the air and producing a forward thrust. If you were to concentrate on the end of one of the blades as the aircraft is flying, the spiral course asserted by the Wrights would be produced.

Wind tunnel testing on airfoils had provided the Wrights with data that would be useful in a propeller design, but it was not so simple to apply. The speed at which the propeller met the air varied along the length of the blade. The tip was moving the fastest and the portion closest to the hub the slowest. To produce an efficient propeller, meant the blade curvature should not be like the simplified one shown in the illustration being fixed at forty-five degrees, but should be tapered, with the portion closer to the hub at a large angle and gradually tapering to a small angle at the tip. Also, the blade width could vary along its length, so the design of the propeller was a very complicated process.

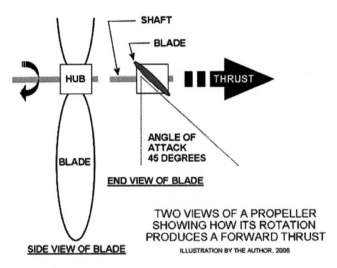

Figure 7-1. A properly designed propeller turned by a shaft will produce a thrust forward that varies approximately as the square of the rotational speed. [Illustration by the author, 2006]

By mid-1903 they had worked through many problems, and arrived at a procedure to produce an efficient propeller. As historian Peter L. Jakab wrote, "In a letter to George Spratt, Orville shared the latest developments with a clever turn of phrase that succinctly illustrates the brothers' typical method of approaching a problem, as well as their burgeoning self-confidence concerning eventual success."[9] Orville wrote:

We had been unable to find anything of value in any of the works to which we had access, so that we worked out a theory on our own on the subject, and soon discovered, as we usually do, that all propellers built heretofore are *all wrong*, and then built a pair of propellers 8-1/8 feet in diameter based on our theory, which are *all right!* (till we have a chance to test them down at Kitty Hawk and find out differently). Isn't it astonishing that all these secrets have been preserved for so many years just so we could discover them!! Well our propellers are so different from any that have been used before that they will have to either be a good deal better, or a good deal worse.[10]

The propellers preformed better than any heretofore built. Orville reported, "Our first propellers built entirely from calculation, gave in useful work [a thrust equal to] 66 per cent of the power expended. This was one about third more than had been secured by Maxim or Langley."[11] The Wright brothers had solved the complicated design problem.

Drive Chain Design

It was decided to use two propellers spinning in opposite directions to neutralize the gyroscopic action so as not to introduce a so-called "turning moment" into the aircraft. Also two propellers would "secure a reaction against a greater quantity of air, and at the same time use a larger pitch angle than was possible with one propeller."[12]

The motor was mounted alongside the pilot, mitigating the possibility of causing injury to the operator should there be a head-on crash. The motor drove each propeller by a chain, with one of the chains housed in tubing and crossed to produce a rotation in the opposite direction. The drive chain was tested in Dayton and they found the tubing used in the propeller shafts were too weak, so thicker tubing was substituted.

Strut Redesign

Recognizing that engine power consumed in overcoming drag would incrementally diminish their chances of powered flight, the Wrights resumed wind tunnel testing in early 1903. On February 2, Wilbur reported the somewhat surprising results to Chanute. Orville, several months later, communicated much of the same information to Spratt, providing him the strut cross-sections shown in figure 7-2 along with the drag data therein.

The most startling result was that rounding the front edge of the strut actually increased the resistance to air to one hundred and five percent, while rounding the back edge reduced it to forty-five percent. Rounding both edges achieved another reduction to thirty-five percent. By making the front pointed and the back rounded, the structural integrity of the strut decreased and the drag increased to fifty percent.

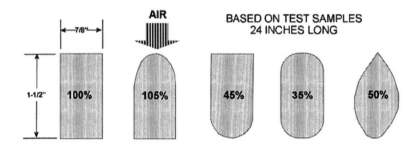

Figure 7-2. Shown are five different strut cross-sections tested. The rectangular one on the left was the baseline, normalized to 100%. [Illustration by the author from electronically tracing the images from Orville's letter of June 7, 2003 as found in the Library of Congress.]

Based on theses results, Orville told Spratt, "We are building the new uprights with rounded corners." Orville noted that Chanute favored the fish shape (far right), and he "seems to very seriously doubt the accuracy of the measurement."[13] The Wrights, however, had found their 1902 glider performed according to the predicted results derived from wind tunnel testing of airfoils, and would again rely on their own collected data and not on the guess of others.

Controlled testing, keen observation, and collecting and analyzing data to guide new designs were the important hallmarks of the Wrights' engineering approach.

Rib Design

Previously, the ribs had been made of ash that was heated and bent to the desired curvature. After cooling, they generally retained their shape but over time had a tendency to flatten out and this was made worse as the payload weight on the glider was increased. As the 1903 model would have to carry an even greater weight and have a longer rib (6.5 feet), the Wrights decided to produce a design that mitigated or almost eliminated this flattening-out problem.

It was decided to use a compound approach where two thin layers of wood would be held apart by spacers and the assembly glued together as shown in figure 7-3.

The spars that connect the ribs together and provide the lateral strength for the wing are shown in black. Orville noted, "We wrap the ribs at all places where the blocks [spacers] are put in with glued paper, which add greatly to the strength."[14]

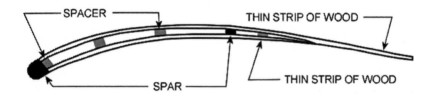

Figure 7-3. Two thin wooden strips, top and bottom, are separated by four spacers (shown gray) to create a rib that would not change shape over time. Imbedded in the rib were the leading edge spar and a spar about two-thirds of the way back. [Illustration by the author, electronically traced from a drawing by Orville in a June 7, 1903 letter to Spratt as found on the Library of Congress website.]

Address to the Engineers

By invitation of Chanute, Wilbur made his second address before the Western Society of Engineers on June 14 in Chicago. The written account of his remarks read in a matter-of-fact manner without the insight provided in his previous address of September 1901. He mentions the adverse yaw problem and the solution implemented by making the tail moveable; and that they had been able to make about one thousand glides, but this had only amounted to five minutes of flying – too short to gain real competence.

Wilbur did provide a calculation to fly the glider at eighteen miles per hour, with one and one-half horsepower, increasing to two horsepower for a speed of twenty-five miles per hour. All in all it was a lackluster performance, as his mind appeared preoccupied with getting everything done to achieve powered flight in 1903.

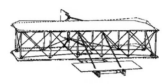

Design of a New Flyer

With the addition of a gasoline engine, fuel tank and fuel, propellers, and power drive chain, the Wrights realized the airframe must be larger and consequently heavier. Wilbur sketched out three views of the craft (with some details missing) using black pencil on brown kraft paper, creating a document that is very difficult to read, especially when reproduced. An electronically reconstructed version is found in figure 7-4.

Unfortunately, Wilbur partially overlapped the top view with the side view so in this area the presentation cannot be accurately portrayed. Many of the components have been annotated to provide a more complete description.

The piece parts for the flyer were being fabricated during the summer and early fall. On September 9, Wilbur wrote to Chanute, "Our preparations for our trip to Kitty Hawk are nearly finished. We shipped some goods today and will ship [the] balance next week. We hope to start ourselves by the 20th." He had previously invited Chanute and Spratt to Kitty Hawk, but wanted no one else present up to the moment of trial, saying, "We have much to do, and so little time to do it in."[15] Wilbur was clearly a man on a mission and needed to stay focused to get everything completed before the onset of bad weather.

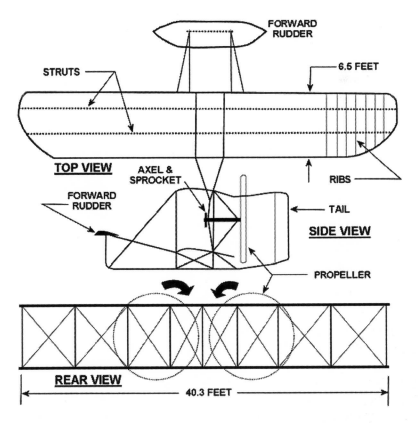

Figure 7-4. A recreation of Wilbur's preliminary three-view sketch of the 1903 flyer is shown. The original sketch is mounted on cardboard and can be found in the Franklin Institute, Philadelphia. [Electronically traced and annotated by the author, 2006, from a photograph in McFarland, *Papers*, opposite page 358.]

Construction at Kitty Hawk

"We reached camp Friday noon, having come over from Manteo in a small gasoline launch," wrote Orville to Katharine on Saturday, September 26. "We found everything in pretty good shape. The building, however, is several feet nearer the ocean than when we left last year, and about a foot lower, in places." A storm with winds up to 107 miles per hour, "beating anything within the memory of the oldest residents" had blown it off the foundation.[16]

Their tools and supplies along with the lumber to be used in the construction of a new building for the 1903 flyer were already there. By the following Monday, the brothers set about erecting the new hanger with inside dimensions of forty-four feet long, sixteen feet wide and nine feet high. Wilbur wrote to Chanute on the first day of October, reporting we "hope to have it finished in a few days more."[17]

When conditions for gliding were favorable, they would forego construction duties and carry their 1902 machine to one of the hills and fly it down. Wind was so perfect, they were able to log many flights and retool their skills at piloting in preparation for the forthcoming heavier flyer.

By October 8, the last shipment of parts for the 1903 flyer had arrived and assembly of the upper surface commenced the following day. It was finished by the 14th and shortly afterward Orville wrote to Milton, "We completed the upper surface of our new machine yesterday. It is the prettiest we have ever made, and of a much better shape, being smooth on both the upper and lower sides."[18] He enclosed a sketch of the 1902 spar protruding from the lower ribs and the improved 1903 embedded spar design (see figure 7-5).

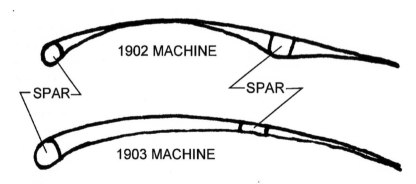

Figure 7-5. Shown is a comparison of the ribs of the 1902 and 1903 machines and the methods used to attach the spars. [From McFarland, *Papers*, page 363, annotated by the author, 2006.]

At this time, the brothers learned via a newspaper report that the test flight of the Langley *Aerodrome* had been a failure. The aircraft, with a fifty horsepower engine, had sped along a launching track, but upon reaching the end nosedived into the water. Langley was a proponent of a self-stabilized airframe, and his reputation would suffer as a result of the failed demonstration.

Wilbur wrote to Chanute on October 16, notifying him their flyer construction plans were behind schedule and it appeared the machine would not be complete until nearly November 1. He added, "I see Langley has had his fling, and failed. It seems to be our turn to throw now, and I wonder what our luck will be."[19] There was no question mark ending the sentence – Wilbur was quietly confident the flyer design was sound and success was only a short time away.

Problems with Propeller Shafts

Spratt arrived on October 23 to assist the brothers and by early November the engine and propellers were being mounted on the flyer (see figure 7-6). A test run on November 5 revealed a number of problems, the most serious of which was the tubular shafts for the propellers were too thin. It readily became apparent that major repairs would have to be made "thus taking away all chance of a trial for ten days or so." Facing an uncertain delay, Spratt decided to leave the camp, and agreed to take the shafts to Norfolk and express them to Dayton along with repair instructions for Charles Taylor.

Chanute arrived the next day about four o'clock, bringing with him, it seemed, cold weather and a blowing wind. During the following week some gliding was attempted with the 1902 machine without much success. There was, however, some progress in fine-tuning the balking gasoline engine. Orville noted in his diary for November 9 "Spent most of the day working on engine and magneto, which after much trouble were got into shape for running. The vibration at high speed is not at all disagreeable."[20]

With bad weather plaguing the project and no news as to when the repaired shaft would be returned, Chanute left the camp on November 12. Three days later a letter was received from Taylor that the shafts had been shipped by express. Orville, writing to his father and sister the same day, reported "This past week and a half has been a loaf, since we have almost nothing to do on the machine until the shafts come. The weather has been fairly cold at times but with a half cord of wood on hand we have not suffered any."[21]

Figure 7-6. The 1903 flyer is shown outside the assembly and storage building, with one of the Wright brothers standing inside. [Wright brothers photograph from the Library of Congress.]

The repaired shafts were received about noon on November 20 and installed after dinner that day. The difficulty of keeping the sprockets tight returned, however. The next day Orville recorded in his diary, "After many attempts to fasten sprockets we finally succeeded by filling thread with [Arnstein's hard] tire cement." With that problem solved the drive chain was tested but the motor ran "irregularly, jerking the chains, and shaking the machine terribly." The new problem was traced to vibrations in the gasoline feed line, which when properly secured the problem went away. A pull test found the propellers could thrust at "132 to 136 lbs. at a speed of 350 revolutions per min," and this greatly restored their confidence in success.[22]

On Monday, November 23, the boys spent time readying the rails for launching the flyer down an eleven-degree slope of Big Hill. A test run to ascertain the amount of gasoline consumed by the engine concluded the amount held by their small tank should operate the machine for eighteen minutes. The same day Orville wrote their mechanic, Charles Taylor, "After a loaf of 15 days, we are down to work again. . . . You did a most excellent job of brazing, and we are highly pleased that the bearings were not injured at all."[23]

Tuesday, the tail attachment was completed and the machine was rolled outside the building, where the center of gravity was measured. The next day additional tests preparatory to flying were run, but a "drizzling rain" starting at noon delayed a trial. Cold weather over the next two days, including "some snow" on Friday, kept the boys inside.

By Saturday November 28 the weather "turned some warmer" and the engine was fired up. After a number of test runs, however, a problem was noted and traced to a cracked propeller shaft. The shafts had been made from tubing to save weight, but the walls were too thin to withstand the vibrations introduced by the motor, drive chain and propellers. They immediately arranged for Orville to return to Dayton and fabricate new shafts, this time of solid spring steel.

Powered Flight at Last

Wilbur held down the camp until Orville returned a week and a half later early the afternoon of Friday December 11. The next day the new shafts were installed and the machine was ready for a test flight, but the wind was not strong enough to start from a level surface and they did not have enough time to go to the Big Hill.

Monday morning was spent readying the launch and "At half past one o'clock we put out [a] signal for station men, and started for hill, which took us about 40 minutes." Bob Westcott, John T. Daniels, Tom Beacham, W. S. Dough and Uncle Benny O'Neal responded and helped take the machine one hundred fifty feet up the incline.

Orville recorded in his diary, "We tossed up a coin to decide who should make first trial, and Will won." Wilbur reported the results to his sister and father later that day:

> We gave the machine first trial today with only partial success. The wind was only 5 miles an hour so we anticipated difficulty in getting enough speed on our short track (60 ft.) to lift. We took to the hill and after tossing for first whack, which I won, got ready for the start. The wind was a little to one side and the track was not exactly straight downhill which caused the start to be more difficult than it would have been otherwise. However the real trouble was an error in judgment, in turning up too suddenly after leaving the track, and the machine had barely speed enough for support already, this slowed it down so much that before I could correct the error, the machine began to come down . . .[24]

85

Figure 7-7. Wilbur is shown on the damaged flyer after the flight of December 14, 1903. [Wright brothers photograph from the Library of Congress.]

Despite the failure that produced some minor damage to the front rudder, Wilbur exuded confidence, continuing, "There is no question of final success."

The next day and a half was spent in making repairs and they were ready to try again by noon of the 16th, but not enough wind was stirring. The next day, however, the wind was blowing twenty to twenty-five miles per hour, so the signal for the men at the life-saving station was hoisted. Before the boys were quite ready, John T. Daniels, W. S. Dough, A. D. Etheridge, W. C. Brinkley and Johnny Moore arrived.

It was now Orville's turn. At 10:35 he released the restraining wire, and with Wilbur running at the side holding the wing level, he lifted off the ground and ascended – carrying with him their sought after dreams and hopes of fame. At this dramatic moment, John Daniels, positioned by the Wrights' camera, snapped one of the most famous and recognizable photographs ever recorded (figure 7-8).

Figure 7-8. Man's first heavier-than-air flight with Orville at the controls and Wilbur standing at the right. This was the final definitive proof that the design approach and calculations done by the Wrights were capable of achieving first flight. [From the Library of Congress website.]

The brothers took turns with three more flights, each beating the previous record. The sensitivity of the forward rudder was too high making it difficult to maintain level flight. Their first four history-making attempts are depicted in figure 7-7.

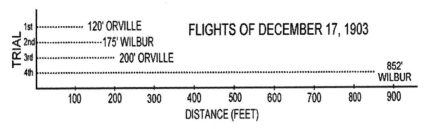

Figure 7-7. Flight trials of the Wright brothers on December 17, 1903 are shown. [Illustration by the author, 2006.]

The fourth trial by Wilbur had lasted fifty-nine seconds but upon landing "the rudder frame was badly damaged." The rudder was removed and the flyer was taken back to the camp and set down a few feet from the building. Without warning, a sudden gust of wind started to roll the machine over, and despite their efforts to restrain it, the machine flipped over, suffering significant damage. This signaled the end of the flying season, but success had been achieved.

Orville sent a telegram home to 7 Hawthorne Street advising his Milton and Katharine, "Success four flights thursday morning all against twenty one mile wind started from Level with engine power alone average speed through air thirty one miles longest 57 seconds inform Press home Christmas."

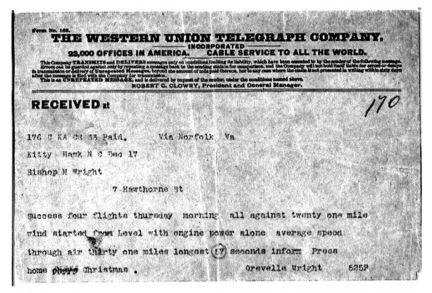

Figure 7-8. The telegram sent by Orville to his father announcing the successful flights of the powered flyer. [From the Library of Congress website.]

Despite the damage to the 1903 flyer, the brothers had accomplished what they set out to do, and in doing so would later be recognized as the inventors of the airplane. There was still more work to be done, a patent to secure, more skeptics to convince, improved models to build, but the trials of December 17, 1903 marked the beginning of heavier-than-air powered flight – ushering in the world of aviation as we know it today.

The 1903 flyer is shown outside the hanger with the Wright brothers standing in front of the aircraft's wings. [From the Library of Congress.]

[1] Tom Crouch, *The Bishop's Boys: A Life of Wilbur and Orville Wright* (New York: W. W. Norton & Co., 1989), p. 245.

[2] Marvin W. McFarland, ed., *The Papers of Wilbur and Orville Wright* (1953, reprint; New York: McGraw-Hill, 2001), p. 299 n.

[3] Ibid., p. 307n.

[4] Orville Wright, *How We Made First Flight*, (Washington: Federal Aviation Administration, 1986), p. 10.

[5] Orville and Wilbur Wright, "The Wright Brothers' Aëroplane," *The Century Magazine* (September 1908) 76:648.

[6] McFarland, *Paper.* p. 292.

[7] Orville and Wilbur Wright, "The Wright Brothers' Aëroplane," *The Century Magazine* (September 1908) 76:648.

[8] Orville Wright, *How We Made First Flight*, p. 8.

[9] Peter L. Jakab, *Visions of a Flying machine: The Wright Brothers and the Process of Invention* (Washington: Smithsonian Press, 1990), p. 196.

[10] McFarland, *Papers*, p. 313. The reference to testing at Kitty Hawk did not infer a lack of confidence in the design, but likely validation.

[11] Orville and Wilbur Wright, "The Wright Brothers' Aëroplane," pp. 648–649.

[12] Orville Wright, *How We Made First Flight*, p. 10.

[13] McFarland, *Papers*, p. 314. There is some small variation of this data provided by Orville and that provided by Wilbur to Chanute. The author relied primarily on Wilbur's data found on page 297 of McFarland, *Papers*.

[14] McFarland, *Papers*, p. 313 n.

[15] Ibid., pp. 353, 355.

[16] Ibid. p. 356.

[17] Ibid., p. 359.

[18] Ibid., p. 363 n.

[19] Ibid., p. 364.

[20] Ibid., p. 378.

[21] Ibid., p. 381.

[22] All paragraph quotes ibid, p. 384.

[23] Ibid., p. 385.

[24] Ibid., pp. 392–393.

Chapter 8

Securing a Legacy in a Competitive World

Nothing is invented and
perfected at the same time.

– John Ray, *English Proverbs*, 1670

Their December 17, 1903 telegram from Kitty Hawk had promised "home Christmas" and a joyous Dayton reunion it was. They were, however, at a crossroads in life. Having achieved their goal of first flight of a heavier-than-air machine, they were faced with the decision to continue the development, or go back to the bicycle business and rest on their laurels.

Their resolve to pursue work on their invention was later explained in a letter to the Aero Club of America, which had requested pictures and models for an exhibit. Wilbur elucidated:

> When my brother and I began experimenting in 1900 it was purely for the pleasure of it. We did not expect to get back a cent of the money we spent. Consequently we agreed with each other that it should under no circumstances be permitted to infringe upon the time and money needed for our business. . . .
>
> But after several seasons we found ourselves standing at a fork in the road. On the one hand we could continue playing with the problem of flying so long as youth and leisure would permit but carefully avoiding those features which would require continuous effort and the expenditure of considerable sums of money. On the other hand we believed that if we would take the risk of devoting our entire time and financial resources we could conquer the difficulties in the path to success before increasing years impaired our physical activity. We finally decided to make the attempt but as our financial future was at stake [we] were compelled to regard it as a strict business proposition until such time as we had recouped ourselves. From first to last our experiments have been conducted entirely at our own expense, and up to the present not one cent of financial return has been received. We shall endeavor to secure our pay in such a way as will permit the world in general to receive the benefit of the invention within a reasonably short time, with the least possible restriction on progress.[1]

Therefore, the Wrights agreed to provide photographs to the club, but believed their time had to be spent securing their old age. Their focus for the future became perfecting the flying machine and turning it into a practical device, which along with its underlying knowledge, could be used to produce a profit – the American capitalistic dream.

Patent Application

In 1903 Wilbur had submitted an application to the U.S. patent office, but it was rejected with advice from the examiner that they obtain the services of an experienced patent attorney. Through friends, they found Henry A. Toulmin, who had an office in nearby Springfield, Ohio, and he agreed to handle the application. Because it would take considerable time to secure the patent, Toulmin "advised saying as little as possible about their invention."[2]

A patent application had to be crafted in a fairly rigorous format containing sections addressing the description, drawings (see figure 8-1), and claims. The concept being patented must be new or novel and not here-to-fore known, so if word leaked out about how they achieved their flying success, there was the real chance the patent would not meet this important test and could be rejected.

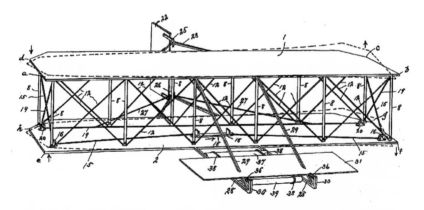

Figure 8-1. One of the five patent drawings of the Wright's flying machine is shown. Note the many callouts (numbers and letters), which had to be explained in the description. [From patent no. 821,393, May 22, 1906.]

The Wright brothers' natural propensities were already not to divulge any critical information. Coupling this with the patent attorney's advice, they were driven to a much higher level of secrecy. This confidentiality would negatively impact selling the aircraft, making it difficult to work out contracts with potential buyers, who were naturally suspicious because flying was so new.

Another recommendation apparently made by Toulmin was to patent the 1902 glider rather than the 1903 flyer. In the overall interest of maintaining secrecy, there would be an advantage to keeping inquiring minds away from the invention; therefore they should make the "application on the soaring machine instead of flying, in order to avoid [the] necessity of demonstrating operation of machine before examiners."[3] From a practical standpoint, should demonstrations be necessary this could lead to more questions, more written response, more time, and consequently more money.

It would be two more years before the patent would be finalized, but when it finally was issued on May 22, 1906 there were a whopping eighteen claims, which carefully covered the aircraft configuration, the three-axis control, and the construction techniques. It would prove to be a good and defensible document and contained the all-important claim of wing warping, which was later judged by the court to be the invention of the aileron.

1904 Flyer Number 2

They began work on a new aircraft in January 1904, and secured the right to use a one-hundred-acres cow pasture eight miles northeast of town. Called Huffman Prairie, this new flying field was near Simms Station, a trolley stop of the Dayton, Springfield & Urbana interurban trolley, so it could be easily reached.[4]

They built a virtual replica of the 1903 machine and installed a new gasoline engine capable of producing 25 to 30 horsepower.[5] It was more powerful than the earlier modes, but also weighed more – two hundred forty pounds when fully fueled and ready to fly. A demonstration for the press without cameras was scheduled for May 23, but engine problems, bad weather, no headwind, and finally a paltry flight of only twenty-five feet provided little opportunity for favorable print-press coverage.

In June a few flights were made and on July 1, Wilbur reported to Chanute, "all the experiments with our 1903 and 1904 machines having shown that the center of gravity was rather too far forward, we decided to shift the engine, man, and water tank to the rear."[6] The change did not work as planned as he later wrote:

> "We shifted the center of gravity backwards as mentioned in a previous letter but the result was not satisfactory. We are now engaged in reconstructing some parts and think we will thus stop the tendency to undulation which has marked our flights with power machines. It will probably be two weeks before another trial is made.[7]

Aviation expert Fred Culick acknowledged "Hindsight is always a satisfying advantage for historical commentary" and made this observation about their difficulty: "they continually fought the pitching undulations . . . [and] in an effort to correct the problem they moved the engine, its water tank and the pilot aft, *exactly the wrong direction*."[8]

Intuition or a "gut feeling" is a necessary and extremely valuable characteristic for an engineer. When this turns out to be completely wrong, as was the case for the Wrights' center of gravity experiment, it is time to put the pencil to paper and analyze what is going on. To avoid the undulations, the pitching moment, m, had to be zero and as Culick notes, the Wrights "never wrote the equation arising from $m = 0$ and therefore had no basis for exploring its implication." He recognizes "their powers of observation and interpretation of the behavior of their aircraft in flight were remarkable."[9] They were not theoretical analysts, however, just very talented and capable empirical engineers who eventually prevailed in solving or mitigating critical control problems by very keen observation, determination, and hard work.

Launching the Flyer

Unlike Kitty Hawk, there was little headwind that could be used to augment the forward speed of the aircraft when getting the machine aloft. They needed longer takeoff runs and with bumpy terrain this had to be achieved with laying more and more feet of track or rails. Keeping the pieces of rail aligned was a major problem. On Monday August 8, Wilbur reported to Chanute:

During July we made but two trials of the Flyer No. 2, and they were of more value for the lessons they taught than for exhibition purposes. After reconstructing some parts of the machine we resumed practice last week and made two trials Tuesday, two on Thursday, two on Friday and three Saturday. One of the Saturday flights reached 600 ft., which is the best we have done with the new machine so far. We have found great difficulty in getting sufficient initial velocity to get real starts. While the new machine lifts at a speed of about 23 miles, it is only after the speed reaches 27 or 28 miles that the resistance falls below the thrust. We have found it practically impossible to reach a higher speed than about 24 miles on a track of available length, and as the winds are mostly very light, and full of lulls in which the speed falls to almost nothing, we often find the relative velocity below the limit and are unable to proceed. [10]

Their solution subsequently worked out was to use a twenty-foot tower and a weight approaching one ton, which was hoisted aloft.[11] The pilot could release the weight that was connected to a rope. The other end of the rope, through a series of pulleys and gears, would catapult the machine down a sixty-foot rail, sending it aloft. With the takeoff problem reasonably solved, the Wrights could focus more on learning how to fly.

Figure 9-2. One of the Wright flyers at Huffman Prairie is shown in June or July 1904. [From the Library of Congress, cropped, cleaned-up and enhanced by the author.]

During August they had made twenty-five starts and flew more than 1,200 feet four times with Wilber noting, "These are about as long as we can readily make on our present grounds without circling."[12] On September 20, Wilbur made the first completed circle with the 1903/04 design, flying more then four thousand feet. Six days later he recorded in his diary a new difficulty that had surfaced, which Culick has analyzed and explained:

> As they continued practicing turns, both Brothers encountered a new serious problem that they characterized as "unable to stop turning" those flights sometimes terminated by crashes. Evidently the cause was one now familiar: stalling of the inner wing of the turn due to its slower speed and higher angle of attack. The Wrights sensed the cause and correctly eased the problem by adding seventy pounds of steel ballast to the canard [forward horizontal rudder] a move that reduced the amplitude of the pitch undulations, and also caused them to fly faster.[13]

When the flying season ended they had made one hundred and five starts and, as their flying skills steadily improved were gradually learning how to turn the machine. The wing warping and control of the vertical tail were interconnected for all of these trials, but in a summary of the experiments in 1904, Wilbur was beginning to understand some problems this was causing.[14] When flying resumed in June 1905, the controls were independent.

1905 Flyer Number 3

When their flight-testing continued the following year, they now had three controls to operate: a lever in one hand actuated the forward horizontal rudder, the other hand moved the vertical aft tail, and their hips controlled the wing warping. The initial trials primarily ended in crashes, as they had to learn how to operate the controls in a coordinated manner to properly fly the aircraft. Wilbur reported to Chanute, "We are sure they will be a good thing when we have learned the combination properly, but they have cost us several rather unlucky breakages, aggregating several weeks of delay."[15]

This time they did some analysis, preparing data on the center of pressure for two of their airfoils, and through more testing they made changes to the sizes and hinging of the forward horizontal rudder and aft tail rudder. Gradually control over the machine was acquired and by September 6 they made "four rounds of [the] field" landing at the starting point.

Stalling or losing control on tight turns continued to plague them even with the new controls. A change in the flying procedure corrected this problem. Wilbur explains:

> When it was noticed that the machine was tilting up and sliding towards a tree, the operator turned the machine down in front and found that the apparatus then responded promptly to lateral control. The remedy was found in the more skillful operation of the machine and not in a different construction.[16]

This solved the last remaining control problem, leading Wilbur to summarize in the 1905 results, "we had discovered the real nature of the trouble . . . [and] we felt we were ready to place the flying machine on the market."[17] Furthermore, flights of more than twenty miles, had been made revealing over-heated transmission bearings, but these were easily corrected. A practical flying machine was at hand; the remaining challenge was to find a buyer.

Selling is Harder Than You Think

The old saying attributed to Ralph Waldo Emerson, "If a man can write a better book, preach a better sermon, or make a better mousetrap than his neighbor, though he builds his house in the woods, the world will make a beaten path to his door," was not true for the Wrights. They clearly had invented a new machine, which portended radical changes for warfare and global transportation, but the governments of the United States, Great Britain, France, and Germany were not quick to act.

From the Wright's vantage point their offer was exceedingly logical. In a May 28, 1905 letter to Chanute, Wilbur wrote:

> We stand ready to furnish a practical machine for use in war at once, that is, a machine capable of carrying two men and fuel for a fifty-mile trip. We are only waiting to complete arrangements with some government. The American government has apparently decided to permit foreign governments to take the lead in utilizing our invention for war purposes. We greatly regret this attitude of our own country, but seeing no way to remedy it, we have made a formal proposal to the British Government and expect to have a conference with one of its representatives, at Dayton, very soon. We think the prospect favorable.[18]

Several months later, however, on October 9, 1905, not hearing from the British and wanting to give the United States another chance, the Wrights wrote to the President of the Board of Ordnance and Fortification of the War Department. The letter referenced the informal offer made "some months ago" and this time proposed to furnish an airplane under contract to be paid for only after trials and the cost would be based on performance. If the aircraft failed to achieve a trial of "at least twenty-five miles at a speed of not less than thirty miles an hour," no obligations would incur.[19]

Government officials, entrusted with the public's money, are reluctant to obligate resources to anything that cannot be fairly well nailed down and are also reticent to take risks that cannot be quantified to the total and complete satisfaction of short-necked bureaucratic bosses. Samuel P. Langley had succeeded in getting $50,000 for his *Aerodrome* experiment and with its failure; there was enough egg to spread around the faces of War Department officials. Besides, others claimed they could also fly and only needed governmental financial support to jumpstart their projects. Government boys were understandably wary about a new venture that some even argued was impossible.

The Wrights, of course, absolutely knew otherwise, hence there existed a real communication gap that would take time to work through. A series of letters was exchanged, but no real progress made toward signing a contract. This took a fortuitous change for the better in the summer of 1907 when Orville was in Paris trying to work out a French contract and was introduced to Lt. Frank P. Lahm, who was there recuperating from a relapse of an earlier bout of typhoid fever. Lahm would soon return to America, assigned to the aeronautical section of the U.S. Army Signal Corps.

Prior to his departure he wrote to the Chief Signal Officer, Brig. Gen. General James Allen, second-highest ranking member of the Board of Ordnance and Fortification, carefully couching a suggestion, "I have to inform you that I have just had an interview with Mr. Orville Wright of Dayton, Ohio, in regards to the purchase of the aeroplane invented and successfully operated by himself and his brother, Mr. Wilbur Wright. It seems unfortunate that this American invention, which unquestionably has considerable military value, should not be first acquired by the United States Army."[20]

One of the major sticking points was the $100,000 price the Wrights were asking and after discussion between the brothers, it was agreed to reduce this to $25,000. Realistically, negotiations were not going well with the French, Germans, or British and if the U.S. was interested in their invention, they would be flexible. Wilbur would later visit with members of the board, who were favorably impressed and found a way to budget the money for them to acquire their airplane.

The contract, however, would not be awarded sole source. The Army would prepare an invitation for bid with the specifications and requirements written around the Wrights' design. To keep crank bidders from responding, they would require that ten percent of the proposed contract price be submitted by certified check with the bid and forfeited in case of failure. By the February 1, 1908 deadline forty-one bids were received ranging from $850 to more then one thousand times that, up to $1 million. One from a federal prisoner promised an airplane in exchange for his release. Another was willing to sell the plane for $45 or $65 per pound depending on the model selected. Realistically, however, only three certified checks were submitted, so the remaining bidders were eliminated from the competition.

One proposal came with a check of $100, all the money the bidder had, which limited the contract to $1,000. He later withdrew. This left the Wrights' bid of $25,000 and a lower bid from Augustus M. Herring for $20,000. The Army resolved this dilemma by finding more money and awarding two contracts.

Mission Accomplished

Two former bicycle mechanics from Dayton, Ohio, had achieved what they set out to do: design, build, test, and finally sell their flying machine to support their old age. Unfortunately, Wilbur would die a few years later in 1912, with his father noting:

> In memory and intellect, there was none like him. He systemized everything. His wit was quick and keen. He could say or write anything he wanted to. He was not very talkative. His temper could hardly be stirred. He wrote much. He could deliver a fine speech, but was modest.[21]

INDEX